Forward

In April of 1988, Rev. Floyd Thompkins, Jr. came to Stanford University to interview for the position of the Associate Dean of the Chapel. Little did I know the wealth of dividends were in store for me. The first of these unexpected dividends was the friendship of this godly man whom I met for the first time.

From the beginning it was evident that in this man was the confirmation of intellectual sharpness and spiritual depth, which our time sorely needs. Subsequent encounters during the last four years have verified the original judgment and increased the original hope. And now that this book has been written, I am glad to help introduce it to the potential readers throughout the world.

Despite unparallel advances in the field of technological science, our day is filled with a great deal of fuzzy thinking, especially in the realm of terminal illness, ravaging diseases and untimely deaths. Christianity has been victimized by this scourge of these diseases, not only from those without but also from many within the professed Church. The question, "What is the Christian message?" would evoke a confusing cluster of replies, capable of being reduced to a common denominator: Do well! To put it plainly, the effect of the Christian message is being confused with the message itself.

"Can an Ethiopian change his skin, or a leopard his spots?" In these words the prophet Jeremiah affirms that what the sinner needs is not a law, nor a theology, nor a ethic-valuable as these may be-but a Savior who can change him within and set him in a new relation to God and his fellow man.

The book, By the Pool of Bethesda, is a book about hope responding in a positive way to those wrestling with some devastating diseases such as AIDS, sickle cell, cancer, and drug addiction. By addressing these concerns, the author not only uses good biblical data, but some sound exegetical emphasis and application.

In this challenging book, Floyd Thompkins Jr, shows the relevancy of the Christian message for our generation. More than ever man needs a gospel that brings to him the wisdom and power of God. He needs a Gospel that reaches the foolish, the feeble and the fallen.

The Rev. Dr. Robert L Fairley
Senior Pastor
Saint John Baptist Church
East Palo Alto, California

Update Twenty Years Later

It has been twenty years since I received a phone call asking me to provide pastoral support to a group of men and women who were "suffering" with A.I.D.S. I am forever grateful to those men and women who gave me the gifts of their courage and their honesty. My journeys with these souls lead to many changes in my life and faith. Out of that ministry this book was born. United Campus Ministries at Stanford University published it, with the title It's Moaning Time. Then a small publishing company approached me about publishing it under the title, By the Pool of Bethesda. This book had a humbling array of positive critical reviews but no commercial success. This is not what it was written for. It was written as a testament, memorial and ministry from the people who lived with, conquered and succumbed to life threatening diseases, specifically AIDS and HIV.

Almost from the first reader, this work found its way into the hands of those who were chronically ill or had terminal diagnoses of diseases and conditions other than HIV or AIDS. It turns out that the typology of the disease has very little to do with the experience of living positive and fighting the battle against an intruder in your body which is attempting to take your life.

Over the years there has been a constant stream of notes attesting to the relevancy of this ministry. I am so grateful to everyone for these notes. Many of these came with encouragement to republish the book. It has gone out of print and it became quite expensive to purchase. So, the communities that Bethesda was intended to reach could not access it.

Therefore, I've decided to republish it in the hope that it provides individuals, churches and non-profit agencies a tool to nourish the spirits who support those doing battle with ravenous diseases.

Two additional chapters have been added- *Every Eye that's Shut Ain't Sleep and Every Good Bye Ain't Gone* and *The Word of Their Testimony*. These come from additional experiences with the community of positive and struggling people. These deal with long-term survivors and the challenge to the believer when a faithful brother or sister dies. Additionally, because so many people found it so useful, the group study questions have been updated and expanded.

Again, the purpose of this book is as it was in the first. It is a celebration, an aid and a tool of empowerment for those who have been given a terminal diagnoses and/or suffer from a chronic disease and the people who love them.

Table of Contents

Floyd Thompkins, Jr.

Waiting At Bethesda

> *Sometime after this there was a Jewish festival, and Jesus went up to Jerusalem. Now at the sheep pool in Jerusalem there is a building, called Bethesda in Hebrew, consisting of five porticos; and under these were crowds of sick people – blind, lame, paralyzed – waiting for the water to move; for at intervals the angel of the Lord came down into the pool, and the water was disturbed, and the first person to enter the water after the disturbance was cured of any aliment that he or she suffered from.*
>
> *One man there had an illness that had lasted 38 years, and when Jesus saw him lying there and knew he had been in this condition for a long time, he said, "Do you want to be well again?" "Sir," replied the man, "I have no one to put me in the pool when the water is disturbed; and while I am still on the way, someone else gets in before me." Jesus said, "Get up, pick up your sleeping mat and walk." The man was cured at once, and he picked up his mat and walked away.*
>
> *(John 5: 1-9 KJV)*

In the time that it takes to say five words – your test came back positive – one's whole life can change. The world will never be the same again. The future becomes uncertain and the past becomes a sparkling array of memories. The present becomes a never-ending sea of uncertainty. For sure, life is not over. The doctor, nurse and psychiatrist assures the patient of that. Some even venture to predict how many years longer one has to live. But the plain truth of the matter is that death isn't the issue. The issue is what kind of life is left in the shadow of the destructive powers of sickness.

It happens so quickly. No matter how much one prepares, one never gets over the feeling that in just a few moments everything has changed. Nothing can be taken for granted anymore. Everything matters and nothing matters. One becomes consumed in a world of medical terms and tests. Almost immediately and whole host of new people enter one's life. The search for cures and the disciplines of treatments place one in a strange position of waiting for something, someone or somebody to reverse this awful event.

The man by the pool of Bethesda had made an art of waiting and he was not alone. The Pool of Bethesda was a well–known place of healing. It was not necessarily religious but it was magical. For years, it's hard to say how long, pilgrims traveled to the pool in expectation of healing. This place was a proven place of hope and consummate despair. People knew that there was healing to be had there, but they also knew that they might not get it. Bethesda had a well-deserved mythology and even better known testimonies of healing. Bethesda was not a mythical tale. It was a place of healing. Without a doubt, something went on at Bethesda; Hope had a measure of common sense and reasonable expectation.

All places of healing are as uncertain and certain as Bethesda. Even though they profess to be about the cure of those who reside there, they nonetheless cannot deny the reality that if something wasn't desperately wrong, you would not be there. Like Bethesda, hospitals and health care facilities are good to know about, important for the community, but frightful to those who must visit them. Their corridors and hallways are packed with anxiety and filled with concerned care. In both places, life is given, but death also makes the rounds. Somehow getting to Bethesda or the hospital represents a different stage of the attack against one's mind, body and spirit. It is a battleground of competitive hopes.

By tradition, now by necessity, hospitals are places of people contesting for the same recourses and attention. Everybody in a hospital has the same thing on their minds–getting whatever they need to get well and getting out of there. There is so much desire for wellness and heath that a strange thing happens to faith and hope. They mutate and change shape and direction. At first, the hospital brings a lightening of the burden. So many people are around and available that one becomes enlivened with the promise of healing. The reliance upon one's own strength, one's own God or one's own hope seems less critical.

A visit to the place of healing will at least convince all the doubters of the sincerity and severity of one's illness or pain. Suddenly, one's struggle doesn't seem as solitary. In the beginning, many people come to visit and offer their help and prayers to you in order to battle your enemy of sickness. If one is known to be at Bethesda or the hospital, it is surely serious. So the burdens of hope and healing are somehow changed. The doctors and the caregivers are there to be the objects of hope.

Soon, however, the rules of Bethesda are made manifest. Not only is not everyone healed at Bethesda, but also the angels of mercy are outnumbered by the number of people in need. Unless one has attendants of wealth – people who can look after your rights or doctors who have a light caseload – one may not get one's healing even it is readily available. There is a great difference between a public and private health care facility.

New immune suppressant drugs, a heart transplant, a liver transplant, bone marrow or a critical surgical procedure which requires unique skills are angelic possibilities whose availabilities are affected by skin color, bank accounts, resources in neighborhoods, age and public policy. Your healing may be available, but you may not get it. All but the most stalwart of friends and family eventually stop visiting. The cure is taking longer than they can wait. Therefore, the place of healing becomes yet another place of desperate struggle to maintain one's dignity in the face of a voracious, plundering enemy.

What is most devastating is that a place of healing, more than any other circumstance in the battle of sickness, can affect one's spirit. One's spirit can become infected by something much more devastating than helplessness - self-pity and envy. You are forced to wear the clothes of a "patient", while the anxiety of a sick person swirls inside of you. You are forced to watch people get healed and go home, hear stories of miraculous cures while you yourself sit waiting on your cure. In the face of such medical and spiritual inequities, self-pity presents itself as a viable option. God seems to bless everyone else but you. The doctors, nurses, and health care providers don't seem to be doing as much for you as they are for others. You start noticing, real or imagined, an attitude that wasn't there before. Consequently, one is left with neither God nor humanity as the objects of faith.

There is only one thing more destructive than believing that one cannot be healed, and that is believing that no one wants you healed. Such a state is a deep, aching solitude from which very few people return on their own. The landscape of this emotional state is not depression. It's deeper than that. It is the lowest depth of despair. It is not so much a loss of the will to live, as the insight that those who are supposed to help you become healed lack the desire and the dedication to do their job. It is a betrayal of colossal proportion.

To suffer injustice, abandonment and a feeling of spiritual solitude while one is healthy is often debilitating, but to experience them while one is sick is utterly obliterating. Futility creeps into one's consciousness. The man who sat by the pool at Bethesda was in such a state. For 38 long years this man had sat by the pool. One hopes that his wait was the longest of its kind.

Bethesda, quite apart from everyone's desire to the contrary, had become a cruel place for him to be. The men sat by the pool out of a muted, faint, but still present hope. He would have given up except that he was not suicidal. He was a captive of hope. Like all captives, he despised his jail as well as his jailer. Hope, the possibility of healing, was a cruel torture sickness. Oh, that he could have given up and gone home! Rather, he was forced to hope.

When Jesus approached the man at the pool of Bethesda, he discovered a man afflicted by faith. He found a man suffering with the infection of hope. Jesus approached a person who had to have faith to live, but had no object or person in which to place his faith. He truly was a "patient" – the one whose waiting had become the definition of his life. None other had presented himself so utterly devastated by sickness. Abandoned by friends, burdened with dependency and afflicted with hope, this patient of Bethesda was unreachable by anyone other than God alone. After 38 years of struggling, the patient at the pool of Bethesda had every reason to believe that humanity and God had cruelly forsaken him and doomed him to look upon the absurd comedy of Bethesda.

When Jesus approached him, it must have seemed to him to be just another mean act in a torturous comedy of Bethesda. While the Biblical text does not hint that the patient knew it was Jesus, even if he had it would not have mattered. The man by the pool of Bethesda knew this cruel tactic of being offered hope only to have it snatched away at the last minute. After one has been through the dance of unrequited hope enough times, one no longer believes that it is worth the effort. He wasn't easily convinced to try another remedy or believe in another cure. He was through entertaining the jailer of hope. If he had to wait, he would wait with dignity. One gets tired of taking stool samples, getting blood drawn from your veins, eating tasteless or horrible food and consuming medicines which causes diarrhea and pain in the name of healing which to date seems as far off as when hope first forced you to stoop to such depths. Running after life was much less dignified than waiting on death.

Thus, when the shadow of Jesus fell upon the patient of Bethesda, he was not impressed. It was the Sabbath. The angel never came on the Sabbath and even if he did, well, what did it matter? If Jesus would have walked up to him and declared his healing, not only might the man not have moved, but also he might have laughed. So for the first and only time in the entire New Testament, Jesus asked a sick man if he wanted to be healed.

The question – Do you want to be healed? – While stunningly simple was, in fact astonishingly complicated. Every- time one chases a cure or takes a step of faith, it involves an enormous amount of courage and vulnerability on behalf of the sick person. As much as we don't like to admit it, every human being only has a finite amount of faith and hope. One's will to live or spirit consist of weaving together acceptable beliefs concerning the nature of God, life and the universe. As one begins to question the power of God, the justice of life and the overall fairness of the universe, one's spirit begins to wane. Perseverance and faith becomes replaced by cynicism and futility. It becomes easier to welcome death than fight for life. Therefore, as each hope is dashed, patients become more and more discriminating as to where and in whom they place their hope. Otherwise, all the living could go out of life before death arrives. So what Jesus is asking, in effect, is "Will you take a chance with me?" "Will you believe, just one more time?"

Indeed, unlike Jesus, too many proponents of faith and healing refuse to recognize that a hospital visit or a fervent prayer can be as much a nuisance as a blessing to a patient in need. This is surely the case if one requires some kind of agreement or declaration of faith from a patient before one can do anything for him or her. In fact, in Bethesda, such requirements of faith can be decidedly mean. Rather, one should not be stunned if faith and hope are not present in a patient who has been sitting in Bethesda for a long period of time. The presence of anger, frustration, cynicism and futility is much more understandable. All of the elements were on display in the man's answer.

The man by the pool of Bethesda answered Jesus, not with a "yes" or a "no" but rather, a simple recitation of the futility, frustration and injustice of his waiting. The question is not whether he wanted to be healed, but whether he dared to believe, given all the evidence to the contrary, that either God or humanity wanted him healed. His very presence at Bethesda had answered Jesus' question. All patients want to be healed. The question that is begging to be answered is whether God wants to heal them.

Likewise, the very presence of Jesus at Bethesda answered his question. The presence of a healthy witness of faith and healing among the patients of Bethesda is always an answer to whether God still cares about those sitting by the pool. The continued pilgrimages of Christians into this world of exhausted spirituality signals a resounding "yes" to the question of whether God wants patients to be healed. Even after 38 years, the answer is still "Yes"! Even after humanity has fled and injustice seems to reign with unrepentant arrogance, the answer is still "yes!" Every time a person of faith appears at Bethesda, he or she embodies a singular statement – no, God has not forgotten nor forsaken you!

Of greater importance to the patients of Bethesda than his presence is Jesus' added statement of healing. Jesus not only witnessed that God was still present, but that God was still able. Without so much as a declaration of faith, nor an affirmation of hope from the patient by the pool of Bethesda, Jesus heals the man. The power of hope and faith to bring terror comes when they are seen as a requirement for healing. Therefore, as the inevitable ebb and flow of these two precious elements occur, human beings begin to believe that their ability to have hope or faith is directly related to probability of their healing.

This is why this passage of scripture is written: so that those who are suffering through the long years of waiting patiently by the pool of Bethesda can know that God still is able and present. It is written to witness that God's presence does not depend upon your faith as much as it does God's faithfulness. It is written to affirm all who believe n healing and are the allies of hope. It is written to remind us that our presence, as difficult as it might be, is pivotal to the embodiment of a healing which is not dependent solely upon the hope and faith of a patient by the pool.

This story emancipates both hope and the patient. Both are freed by the affirmation of God's independent desire for healing. The patient is free to hope and doubt without the fear of God's reprisal. Hope is free to become an ally of grace rather than an implement of torture. Even if one has tired of waiting, has become bereft of hope and has become cynical about the desire of the health care system to provide care, God is still present and able. Even if the answers to the questions of whether one has enough belief in life or God to answer yes and even if one dares to believe in healing, this story is written to assure us that God's answer is always yes- God is always present and able. God will never leave Bethesda, and as long as God is present, healing and health are also present and possible for everyone.

Questions and Exercise for Discussion

1. How is your church withstanding the test of sickness and disease? Write down five words which you or each member of your group feel would characterize how you think your church deals with sick people within your community.

2. Administer the confidential survey found on the following page to your group or congregation.

3. Through the survey, determine how many people in your congregation feel supported by the church when they were sick. Ask specific question. (Were you visited? Did a representative of the church come see you? Did anyone try to address your financial needs?

4. Check the results of the survey and discuss what you learned about the way your church or community deals with sick people.

Church Discussion Survey

	Agree	Disagree
This church has enough teaching on healing and sickness.		
This church takes care of its members when we become sick.		
This church makes people who become sick feel spiritually inferior/		
This church gives me spiritual and physical resources for my family when we are going through a battle with sickness.		
The longer sickness last the worse this church us at care for you.		

I believe sickness is from the devil.		
I believe in miracles.		
I believe in that sickness is sometimes a consequence of sin.		
I believe that the day of miracles is over		
I believe that sickness and sin have nothing to do with one another.		
I believe that the church should teach and preach about healing.		
I believe that the Bible is important sick people to read because it has answers.		

What do you want this church to know about your experience with sickness?

It's Moaning Time

In those days Hezekiah fell ill and was at the point of
death. The prophet Isaiah son of Amoz came and said
to him, "Yahweh says this, 'Put your affairs in order, for
you are going to die, you will not live.'" Hezekiah turned
his face to the wall and addressed this prayer to God,
"Ah, God remember, I beg you, how I have behaved
faithfully and with sincerity of heart in your presence
and done what is right in your eyes."
And Hezekiah shed many tears.
Isaiah 38: 1-3

Hezekiah felt sheer unadulterated shock. He never expected to hear such words come from the mouth of an old friend and fellow servant of God. Together, he and Isaiah had been through a lot. Isaiah was the pre-eminent prophet in Israel. Hezekiah was the nation's celebrated king. Never is their wildest dreams did they imagine that they would be standing with one another sharing a conversation of futility.

Neither of these men was used to being powerless. Now both of them were experiencing the shock of being overwhelmed by circumstances that they neither understood nor could control. Hezekiah did not want to die and Isaiah did not want him to die. But, the word of the Lord was that Hezekiah would die soon.

For Isaiah, as a prophet, such a message was difficult to deliver and much more difficult to accept. It was in the aftermath of the death of another king, Uzzaiah, that Isaiah had begun his ministry. The only thing which made sense out of the tragic death of Uzzaiah was that he had had been called to the ministry. Therefore, when God revealed to him this devastating message about the king whom he had grown to respect, he must have been thrust into his own spiritual battle. Even while he struggled to deliver his message, he was seeking some reason why God had sent such a message to Hezekiah.

Why had God chosen him to deliver such a message? Why had God ordained him to see another great man of faith die before his eyes? Never had he so regretted this awful burden of faith and its splendid knowledge that God was in control of things that happened in the world. In every other instance when God had prevailed upon Isaiah to speak God had given him some indication that there was some hope. His prophecies had at times been harsh, but never mean. With every announcement about the loss of a battle came a word of assurance that the war would ultimately be won. But, this word –"You are going to die so prepare yourself "- seemed so final and hopeless. He could not blame some non-descript sickness, but rather he knows that God, either by commission or omission, was in control of what was to happen to his friend, and this made it hurt the more.

It should not be the case, but it is nonetheless is, that for most of us, it is more difficult to accept the death or suffering of someone who loves the Lord or are perceived as a Good person than to accept the death and suffering of someone who does not believe in God, or are perceived as a bad person. For people of faith, a terminal sickness, a ravaging disease and an untimely death are an attack upon the reputation and faith of the whole community of believers. It is not that believers think that they are exempt from death and suffering, but it is nonetheless true that believer's think of himself or herself as blessed with special and protective presence of God. Believers think of themselves as chosen, set apart and on a first-named basis with God. Far too often, when someone who is an open and strong advocate of faith suffers, people presume that he or she did not really believe. They declare that the Lord is somehow pulling the cover off their hypocrisy.

Whether Isaiah believed these things or not, he at least had the decency to not verbalize them. He just delivered the message and stepped back. But even this must have been difficult. He did not attempt to give Hezekiah advice. He resisted the temptation to offer platitudes or vain statements to his friend – the king.

Often, we perceive that God is strangely silent to the prayers of one of our friends or family who is suffering, we believers, will attempt to speak for God. We dare to explain what God has decided to leave a mystery – the reason for the suffering. Believers cannot imagine that God could or would be so silent when one of God's own is asking. Didn't God hear, or wasn't the question phrased correctly? When the silence is long enough or poignant enough the believer comes to conclude, "Surely God has answered. We must simply be having trouble recognizing the answer." So in lieu of a right scripture" or a "strong testimony," pieces of advice are given freely o explain he suffering – advice which is so cruel as to defy any sense of kindness. When this advice is heard in the abstract it is astonishing. Besides being an affront to the faith of the ones who suffer, it is an embarrassment to God. For example, "The Lord must trust you in order to let you have this privilege to suffer for God"; or "Perhaps there is an unconfessed sin which you and the Lord need to get straight," and, "If you had more faith you would be well by now." Sometimes the best gift that a believer can give someone who is sick is silence. Sometimes, like Isaiah =, you have to wait and pray until God chooses to speak.

Isaiah, a man of words, had to learn about the ministry of silence and support. Unless he had a Word from the Lord, his words were a burden, not a blessing. He stepped back from Hezekiah. Whether he was crying or not, the text does not say, but he fell silent before God and his friend.

Hezekiah knew all that Isaiah was going through and did not tempt him or burden him with the questions of "Why not? Or what is God doing? He was considerate of his friend. He knew how hard it must have been. More to the point, Hezekiah knew that Isaiah did not have the answers to his questions. He did not ask more of the prophet than he could give. Some things people cannot do for one another. There are some matters that we must take care of ourselves.

As well as Isaiah knew Hezekiah; he did not know that was most hidden and hurtful in his own heart. Isaiah could not look through the king's eyes and imagine what he dreamed and hoped for – a future – which was not possible. The reality of our lives arrives long after we have experienced them through our hopes and dreams. A parent imagines a child's adulthood when he or she is an infant. A husband and wife imagine the rewards of a retirement together in the midst of the struggle to establish themselves. So many dreams left so unfulfilled. It does not matter that they have not happened. They have happened in the minds and souls of the ones who dreamt them. This, Isaiah's pronouncement to Hezekiah was an alarm that a thief had stolen his most precious possession - his future.

Hezekiah's faith was supposed to guard his future. Only God knew what he had hidden there. It was God that Hezekiah turned and asked his most intimate questions. The king dismissed his servants and turned his face toward the wall to talk to God.

If the Lord was to take him home, Hezekiah demanded a personal explanation or at least an escort. If the Lord was to heal him, Hezekiah knew that it would be on the basis of a direct appeal. He knew others were praying. In fact, he knew that the whole nation was praying. But he did not wish to pray for his body but rather his faith. Hezekiah decided to moan a little while.

As the king of Israel, Hezekiah was steeped in a culture that had a whole tradition about moaning – he lament. Moaning and lamenting are not the same as moaning and wailing. The latter two are done to remember the dead. Moaning and lamenting are appeals to the one who holds life.

Hezekiah turned his face away from those who stood waiting to help him put his affairs in order. He had to moan and lament. He turned to talk to God. The full text of the prayer is rather short. So short that it is hard to believe that the writers of Isaiah have captured the entire text of the prayer. The tradition of lamenting was well established in Hezekiah's culture. Laments had certain well-developed traditional elements. These are, as noted by Bernard Anderson in *Understanding the Old Testament*: an invocation to God, a presentation of complaints, a confession of trust in God, a supplication for help or forgiveness, and a vow that God would be praised anyhow. (p.512) But these elements are not rules. They are observations that a lament or a moan always tended to be a review of the past (I have been faithful), a request for the present (I need you to be faithful to our relationship of the past by healing me now), and a statement for the future (My faith will continue in you because you are faithful, whether you heal me or not).

These prayers are not passive. In and of themselves they represent not only wrestling with God, but wrestling with one's illness. A benefit from belief in God is having a sense, through a relationship with God who created life, that one has some form of control over life. Sickness shatters this illusion. It would be wholly intolerable if sickness replaced God as the greatest power in one's life. To give o much attention and honor to such destructive powers is to live in a world without joy, miracles or optimism. If Hezekiah had to think of his illness he would do so in prayer, not in vain conversations with people who knew no more than he did as to why this had happened to him. He would at least give himself a fighting change by appealing to the God who had fought and won all his battles up to now. Moaning is a way of gaining back a sense of power. Hezekiah was moaning for his life and his faith. He was moaning in search of a new relationship to God. As a sick person, how does one relate to God?

When sickness touches your body, as a person of faith, you have to learn to Praise God again. The language of worship and prayer has to be redefined. The intensity of one's spirituality assumes new dimensions. You just have to moan to rediscover the face of God. You have to develop a new approach to the throne of God by using your old relationship as a guide now instead of a destination. Hezekiah knew that his faith and relationship with God was either going to have to be enough to take him home, or it would be the element that would entice God to heal him.

For this reason, psalms of lament end in songs of praise. Psalm 22 proclaims:

You are the theme of my praise in the Great Assembly; I perform my vows in the presence of those who fear God. The poor will receive much as they want to eat. Those who seek God will praise God. Long life to their hearts!

But such optimism comes from an internal battle with the enemy of depression. When Hezekiah isolated himself he did so with the intent of praise not surrender. The words of his battle are not recorded but the spirit of his commitment is demonstrated by his action of prayer. Prayer can lead to praise only if it is entered into with the determination to not stop until it ends in praise.

Optimism is restored because God is rediscovered in the midst of suffering. God has not abandoned us. God can endure our angry shouts. God can wrestle with the most profound sense of hopelessness and bring hope anew. God can empty the power of loneliness by promising an eternal presence. Surely, goodness and mercy shall pursue after moaning and lamenting.

For Hezekiah, the dawning of the new world included a physical healing. A miracle occurred in his body to match the one that he experienced in his heart, mind and soul. His is a tangible witness that God is affected by moaning and is in the midst of praise.

Graciously God rewarded the patience and wisdom of his praying prophet. The word came to Isaiah that Hezekiah would be healed. He too, was waiting on the Lord with determined prayer and expectation. If his friend would turn his face from him, Isaiah would commit to turn is face toward God with the determination of hearing from the Lord about what he too should do. God restored Isaiah's faith in God's sovereignty. His gift for being obedient to God and praying in silence for his friend was the privilege of participating in the testimony of his friend. Because he had not abandoned his friend and he had obeyed God, Isaiah could rejoice in full measure and sing with certainty that his God was real.

Hezekiah sang his psalm of praise:

What can I say? Of what can I speak to God? It is God who is at work; I will glory to you all the years of my life for my sufferings. It is you who have kept my soul from the pit of nothingness; you have thrust all my sins behind your back. (Isaiah 38:15,17)

It's moaning time! Moaning may not result in physical healing. Too many saints have already departed from this world to make such a claim. But it is not a time to avoid the struggle of sickness or to simply capitulate to its implicit and overt challenges to one's faith or the faith of a whole community. Weeping and wailing are not just tools of death- they also tools of life. Don't be afraid to ask the obvious question: Where is God?" Trust that God will answer. If God does not answer now, when? Hezekiah and Isaiah are the witnesses to the presence of God. If you call on God, God will answer. God hears and responds to mains and laments.

Questions and Exercise for Discussion

1. Read Psalm 22 and Luke 22L 29-32. Are these examples of moaning?

2. Outline Psalm 22 by using the outline that Bernard Anderson outlined. (See page 21)

3. Do you know some secular and religious moaning songs? Share them with your group. Why are they important to you? What do they tell you about getting through hard times? Perhaps sing some of them together.

4. Make list of infuriating things people said to you about your sickness or healing and share them with the group. Why were these statements especially irritating? What would you have rather herd from them? What statements or sentiments would have been helpful?

5. What are ways that you or the group could change challenge or encourage the language that is used around sick people?

Empty Jars and Bills to Pay

The wife of a member of the prophetic brotherhood appealed to Elisha. "Your servant, my husband is dead," she said, "and you know your servant revered God. A creditor has now come to take my two children and make them his slaves."

Elisha said, "What can I do for you? Tell me, what have you in the house?" Your servant has nothing in the house," she said, "except a pot of oil." Then she said, "Go outside and borrow jars from all your neighbors, empty jars, and not too few. When you come back, shut the door on yourself and your sons, and pour the oil into all these jars, putting each aside when it is full."

So she left him; and she shut the door on herself and her sons; they passed her jars and she went on pouring. When the jars were full, she said to her son, "Pass me another jar." "There are no more." Then the oil stopped flowing. She went and told the man of God who said, "Go and sell the oil and redeem your pledge; you and your children can live on the remainder."

II Kings 4: 1-7(KJV)

For people who are poor the presence of sickness, disease or death in one's family often means that a bad situation has only gotten worse. To be poor is to be without what you need to protect yourself from the basic enemies of life. It is to be continually choosing between essential things as if they were luxuries. It is to have the choice of eating or shelter, the choice of clothes or entertainment. It is the choice of who will eat this meal and skip the next three meals. Destitution is even more devastating. Worse than being poor, it doesn't even leave one with the choices between the essentials. The necessities just aren't there. Food, clothing and shelter are completely absent.

In both situations, it seems as if humanity has conspired against poor people or people who are born into destitution. A numbing weariness accompanies both conditions. As one struggle to "rob Peter to pay Paul" find a way to accept a hand out with dignity, an attitude of anger and frustration is created. All who are born poor or are born in destitution know deep within themselves that they are victims of a cosmic injustice. They know that there is no difference between themselves and those who have plenty. They are aware that life itself has become one massive and violent assault against the quality and character of their existence. Poor folk and people in destitution are always struggling against the world around them. And it is a testimony to the human spirit, all things being equal, that people win most of the time. Laughter, joy and fun can be wrestled away from despair and hopelessness.

So it is a particularly cruel event when death, sickness and disease settle in the lives of the poor and those in destitution and threatens to tip the battle between life and death towards the abyss of destruction. An even more violent and sinister act is that sickness; disease and death can bring them the terror of becoming poorer or falling into destitution. These are financial attacks as well as physical attacks. Both battles possess the same terrifying dimensions of destruction for ourselves for ourselves and those whom we love.

The widow and her son had fallen into battle with destitution brought about by the death of her husband. This story is a part of the national epic of a people. Her story appears in a book that has acquired the name of II Kings. This book and the first book of Kings comprise a history of a people from the perspective of those who were religious. The widow's story is a part of a cycle of miracle stories, which establishes the identity of Elisha (I Kings 3:4-8:15) It is also about God's response to destitution and inequality.

The widow's tale is monumentally important, even though it is forgetfully short. She is described as the widow of one of the prophetic brotherhood of Bethel. We never find out her name or the name of her husband. Rather, he is known only by his title and position. We know that she is a woman of some status. She was not used to obscurity. The prophetic brotherhoods were neither poor nor were they especially wealthy. But they did have status. One's position in a healthy society is quite often not determined by wealth, but by job and work. Often, what we do is how we are known.

To lose one's job is to become peculiarly invisible. Our titles, positions, and jobs are so much a part of our identity. They communicate class, status and position. Indeed, jobs are about more than money. They are representing societal acceptance. Some people have taken lower-paying jobs for jobs with higher status. If we are good for nothing else, we can at least work. At the very core, the ability to work represents our most basic form of making a living. It is our most powerful weapon against dependency. The loss of a job or of the ability to work represents a great danger to the ways and means that we live our lives.

In a different way, jobs, titles and positions also produce many of our friends. In sheer time allotment, all of us the working rich, the working poor and those of us in the middle spend much of the day fulfilling our roles assigned to us by our jobs. Despite our best efforts to the contrary, jobs, titles and positions often define much of our feelings of worth. Therefore, the writer's description of the woman as the wife of one of the brotherhood of priests is probably as understandable today as it was when the writer first penned this description.

What may not be as telling (although it probably is more than we would like to admit) is the writer's description of the wife as a widow. Widowhood was a major category of concern for the writers of the history of the Old Testament. The Mosaic laws made widows a protected category in their society. Widows were always women, never men. But it would be misinterpretation to simply say that widowhood was about not having a man in your life. In the rules of this gender-segregated society, men were the legal representatives for a family. He was the one who worked outside the home while she worked outside the home while she worked with the matters of the household. Therefore, much of the identification with status, position and worth that is mentioned above only applied to men. The status of women in this society was derived wholly from men. Even if she wished to work, which many women did, she could not work outside her prescribed boundaries. Men were especially vulnerable to both an inflation of ego and the debilitating weight of worry about financial welfare of their households. Their physical health and emotional involved the welfare of their whole family.

However, this too is not so strange. In segregated society, widowhood was always female. But the only changes that our present pseudo-gender integrated economic systems have brought is that the strains of widowhood, and the worries of the plight of loved ones due to the loss of life or the ability to provide, now weigh equally upon men and women. This is why life, accident and disability insurance policies are seen as a necessity. To die or become incapacitated without providing for your loved ones, whether you are a man or a woman is seen as an almost unforgiveable act. In effect, one disease, illness, or accident can kill a whole household. In a country with no national health care system, such as the US, these risks are almost always on the minds of every worker. The death of one can mean the economic death of many.

This is what the widow experienced with the death of her husband. His death made her poor, and it threatened the welfare of her children. It was a common and legal practice to take children into slavery for the debts of their parents. (Exodus 21:7) Her household of faith had become a household of disgrace. She had been robbed of her sense of security. Death had taken her husband away. Now the bill collectors were about to take her children away. She had much to mourn. Her house had been invaded by the presence of poverty, and she was left alone to face a world with few good options.

Strangely enough, the text does not mention her family. It was a fairly common practice for a widow to join the household of their husband's oldest brother. (See the case of Tamar-Gen 38) Further, because she was a widow, the community should have made provisions to care for her and her children. All the usual systems of compassion and care broke down for this woman. Familial and national support systems were simply not there. This was truly a tragedy. This ensured her position of poverty.

The widow had one remaining resource. Yes, family failed her and her community failed her. But she hoped that the people of faith would not fail her. It was time to appeal to God. She approached the prophet Elisha, who was one of her husband's prophetic brothers. In fact, it may have been the case that Elisha knew her husband. She reminded him of the faith of her household. Regardless of who else had failed her, she expected him and the God he represented to do something. Elisha was stunned by her request. Doubtless, he was surprised to find a widow of the brotherhood in such a position.

It is at this juncture in the story that the writer does a singularly strange thing. The woman is given all the attention. What she is required to do in order to experience her economic miracle is explained meticulously. The writer explains, in great detail, all the elements that she had to assemble. It is clear that Elisha was not present at the time of the miracle. It was only she, her children and a little bunch of barrowed empty jars from her neighbors and a little oil. These are essential elements to stave off unwarranted economic disaster in the time of death, sickness and disease.

To become poor or to fall into the prison of destitution, as the widow fell, one had been radically abandoned by all those who should have cared. All the people, institutions and traditions that she had her husband had upheld in their lifetime had to have left her. Her neighbors had to have become utterly uninvolved with her. The creditor had to believe that she was without recourse.

26

Sickness, disease and death have no power to create destitution unless compassion, care and support flee in the face of their presence. If these are absent, homelessness, malnutrition and vagrancy move in to claim yet another victim. These victims of destitution are always an indication of a failure on someone's part to provide for the needs of the suffering. The presence of poor people and those who fall into the disaster of destitution because of sickness, disease or the death of a loved one is an indication of a larger sickness in that society. Someone, some system has failed them. Sickness, disease and death should not have this power. They possess enough terror.

When Elisha asked," What do you have?" she said, "Nothing but some empty pots and a little oil." She could have just as easily answered that she had nobody who was to be her brother or sister. God must willingly answer for sickness, disease and death, but the community of believers must answer if a widow becomes poor or falls into destitution because of these things. This is what is so hurtful. After giving to others, paying taxes or even paying your insurance premiums, you can still find yourself abandoned. The agencies say that you are not poor enough. The federal government says that it is broke and doesn't have money for research or drugs to combat the disease or sickness that is ravaging your body. The insurance company has hired a lawyer to try to find a loophole to cancel your policy. A massive failure of compassion, justice and fairness is going on. These are not God's fault. So the name of God is never mentioned in the text of the story.

When Elisha hears that the widow has empty jars and a little oil, he instructs her to go to her neighbors and get some of their empty jars. Involve them in this miracle. She and her family are sent out to coerce, cajole and contend for the jars of their neighbors. This is an unfair thing to ask them to do. We are asked to believe that their neighbors gave these poor people empty jars. A skeptic of the miraculous might contend that every jar that they gathered came with a little oil in it. Such that, by the time they had collected all the jars, there was enough oil in them to pay their bills. The ambiguity of the story lends itself to that interpretation. So does common sense, not to mention the Mosaic Law. But the other interpretation, in keeping with the tradition of the writer of this text, is that if common sense does not prevail in one's fellow human beings, and all one receives is empty jars and bills to pay, God will make a way somehow.

Magic, yes! But poor people have to rely upon magic to put food on the table. Because the people of faith do not respond to the needs of the sick, the lack of economic survival in such a time of failure is as much an embarrassment to the faith community as sickness is a challenge to God's claims of love and justice. Oil, in this context, has both an economic interpretation and religious meaning. In the culture of the widow, it was a symbol of the presence of God. The image here is literally one of God pouring God's self out to meet the needs of a servant.

No one should have empty jars in their homes. No one should have their children's lives jeopardized. No one should have to cajole, coerce, and convince his or her neighbors to give him or her some of their abundance. No one should have to prove that they are worthy of compassion. This is one injustice of sickness, disease and death that humanity can do something about. The losses of the ability to work or the bills that arise from medical care are the whole community's responsibility. Neighbors are there to help.

If people only extend jars to a widow, she still has the promise of the oil. The anxiety of the situation is at least met by the faithful presence of God, and fear of destitution is at least balanced with the promise of God's abundance.

Questions and Exercises for Discussion

1. Reread II Kings 4:1-7 and then read Matthew 25: 31-46, as well as Luke 4:14 -21. Discuss the significance the church or an individual's response to poverty as a hallmark of biblically based faith. (Feel free to add other texts to this exercise. The Bible has much to say about poverty and the Faithfull's response to it.)

2. What are the support systems for those who become ill and/or fall into poverty in your communities? After you name these systems of support, identify which ones you have had a hand in creating and maintaining.

3. The preceding chapter mentioned the weakness or absence of a national health care system. Poll your community and find out who among you are particularly vulnerable because of being uninsured or underinsured.

4. How can you and/or your community help fill the empty jars of families in need?

Floyd Thompkins, Jr.

Mary Don't You Weep; Martha Don't You Moan

Now a certain man was sick, named Lazarus of Bethany, the town of Mary and her sister Martha. (It was that Mary which anointed the Lord with ointment, and wiped his feet with her hair; whose brother, Lazarus was sick. Therefore, his sisters sent for him, saying, "Lord behold, he whom you love is sick."

When Jesus heard that, he said, "This sickness is not unto death, but for the glory of God, that the Son of God might be glorified." Now Jesus loved Martha, and her sister and Lazarus...

Then when Jesus came, he found that he (Lazarus) had lain in the grave for four days already. Now Bethany was about fifteen furlongs off and many Jews came to comfort them concerning their brother.

Then Martha, as soon as she head that Jesus was coming, sent and met him, but Mary sat still in the house.

Then Martha said to Jesus, "Lord if you had been here, my brother would not have died. But I know that even now, whatever you ask of God, God will give it to you." Jesus said to her, "Your brother shall rise again..."

...she (Martha) went her way, and called Mary her sister secretly, saying, "the master has come, and he calls for you." As soon as she heard that, she arose quickly and came to him,

John 11: 1-5,17–22, 28–29

Mary and Martha loved one another. But theirs was a tension filled relationship. They were two different people, living under the same roof, bound by one word – sisters. In the New Testament Mary was depicted as the one who anointed Jesus and wiped his feet with her hair. The anointing of his head was normal; the washing of his feet was an intimate, almost romantic sign of profound affection for Jesus (Matt. 26:7; Mark14: 3-9). She was at Jesus' feet, apparently enraptured by every word, which proceeded out of the mouth of the teacher. She bathed herself in the presence of Jesus and was comfortable assuming the freedom, which Jesus gave to women, enabling them to sit with him as he taught,

Martha's relationship with Jesus was based on servitude and obligation. She busied herself with support of the ministry of the household. Whenever Jesus visited she served him and his disciples. She submerged her love by impeccably carrying out her duties as the woman of the household. Unlike her sister, Martha could not accept Jesus' invitation to sit and listen to his teaching. Rather, she was secure in expressing her love for Jesus in the traditional manner of women.

The differences between Mary and Martha did not seem to bother Jesus but it bothered these women. In the gospel of Luke, Martha resents Mary's self-indulgent act of sitting and listening to Jesus when there was work to be done.

[40] But Martha was distracted by all the preparations that had to be made. She came to him and asked, "Lord, don't you care that my sister has left me to do the work by myself? Tell her to help me!"

[41] "Martha, Martha," the Lord answered, "You are worried and upset about many things, [42] but few things are needed—or indeed only one. [a] Mary has chosen what is better, and it will not be taken away from her."

Luke 10:39-42 (NIV)

In this all-too-brief exchange between Jesus, Mary and Martha, one can detect a distinct difference in their roles. It is doubtful that Martha's almost rude indication that her sister was shirking her famine responsibility and filial responsibility resulted from Mary sitting at Jesus feet. Nay, this was a family pattern. Martha resented it but could not resist it. She was the responsible one.

Aside from mothers and fathers, there always seems to be a responsible one. This is a sister or brother who finds himself or herself caring for the household and taking up the slack for everyone else. Sometimes the responsible one is considered domineering. Sometimes he or she is considered presumptuous, attempting to mother or father his or her own brothers and sisters. But, every time there is a crisis, despite the previous protest of siblings, the responsible one is called and inevitability must bear the burden of getting everyone through the situation at hand.

It is the responsible one, who, like Martha, is not allowed to sit, think and even pray. In the time of sickness and disease, he or she must deal with the financial needs of the family. He or she must fill out the insurance forms, negotiate what ought to be told, why ought to be told and how it ought to be told. The responsible one has to meet with doctors, adjust to the needs of the one who is sick and answer the phone calls of the ones who feel guilty. The responsible one has to deal with the tension between friends and family and find a graceful way of turning away visitors who will do more harm than good.

Like Martha, the responsible one is often seen as too busy for his or her own good. Everyone is always telling the responsible one to sit down, take care of yourself. Nonetheless, even as these statements are being made, everyone knows that they do not want them to come true. Even though people might mean them, sometimes one has to be the anchor of the family.

Sickness and disease often have two victims: the one who is physically attacked and the responsible one. The toll upon the latter is less obvious than it is upon the one who is being physically attacked. He or she is the one who is close to the futility of the struggle. He or she is the one left with the feelings of guilt. It is left to the responsible one to perform the excruciating tasks of assuming more and more power over another person's life in order to help that person to die. Consequently, the responsible one often feels as though he or she has been an accomplice in the theft of the life of one's loved one. Everyone knows that somebody must take control of the personal and emotional affairs of the dying, but nobody is comfortable with the one who actually has to make these hard decisions.

Quite often the minds of both the person who is ill and the person's family, the responsible one somehow becomes identified with the disease, instead of with the care, which he or she is extending. While others speak of "trying everything possible," he or she mentions funeral arrangements, wills and last conversations. More than any other member of the family, the faith of the responsible one is questioned. It is sometimes even speculated, in the hearts of some, that the attentiveness to the raw realities of sickness by responsible one bespeaks a lack of faith. Further, that this doubt stands in the way of healing of the one who is sick. In effect, the responsible one is sometimes treated as though he or she were an ally of the illness rather than a warrior on behalf of the one who is sick.

Indeed, the responsible one can understand Martha's rebuff to her sister. Nobody is happy being the responsible one. You wish someone else would do more than sit and look up to Jesus when there is work to be done. It is not that you relish the job of being the responsible one. If only the other members of the family could know how much responsible ones wished to cry, think and pray out loud. They would know that the responsible one is also wounded. In fact, the responsible one usually needs more care and loving than any other member of the family. Still, this person is often left out of the embrace of memories and appreciation that accompany the end of the ordeal.

If death does come, instead of being able to weep and fall exhausted upon the shoulders of others, the responsible one is called upon to become the shepherd of grief for the family. He or she has to make the ceremonial and civil arrangements for the burial and the funeral. Nevertheless, after being the support for everyone else, the responsible one can be left alone, emotionally exhausted and spiritually wounded. The family is closer, you were the one who kept them all together, but you feel left out.

At least, however, for the responsible one, who comes to understand that the loved one is going to die, there may be more ability to get beyond the tragedy. But, for others, whose faith is so unrelenting as to hold onto the exclusion of the possibility of the present sickness ending in death, it is harder to let go, and therefore the pain of the ordeal is far more abiding. Unlike her sister, Mary could never let herself believe that her brother would not be healed. Mary believed in the master's words. The scriptures are unclear as to which sister decided to send for Jesus. But, it is not beyond the scope of probability that it was Mary's idea to seek the master, and that the wording of the message, a notification of Lazarus' sickness without a request for healing, was Martha's.

Mary had faith that Jesus would come and heal her brother. After all, besides being a great healer and a rumored Messiah, Jesus was their friend. But, for whatever reason, Jesus did not come and her brother died. Mary's faith which seemed much stronger than Martha's before the ordeal, proved much weaker after it. Like Jesus' other disciples, Mary understood Jesus' presence as a form of magic. They clearly believed that, as long as they knew Jesus, they would never have to endure unanswered questions, unexplained suffering and the frustrations of limited power.

When Jesus finally did come to Bethany, it was Martha who ran to meet him – not Mary. The two sisters were isolated in their grief and individual in their reactions to Jesus' arrival in Bethany. Mary could not bring herself to come to him. It was not that she had lost her faith; she was just plain angry. Jesus had embarrassed her and let her down. Sickness, disease and death of a loved one will often affect those who believe that their faith is stronger and more acute than those who have little or no faith. Mary simply stayed were she was. She may have literally been frozen by the chill of her own anger and disappointments. More than Martha, Mary had to ask what good are all the words of Jesus if he does not come when you need him?

Mary could not thrust from her mind the questions about Jesus' apparent absence and failure to heal her brother. During most times in our lives our ignorance if God's actions can be explained through words like "mystery" and "sovereignty". However, when it comes to death, we are less able to leave it to the mysteries of God. Rather, we feel betrayal and disappointment. Questions of doubt and a seething anger of betrayal seize us, and we are left paralyzed in our attempt to go on. When Jesus came to Bethany, Mary just sat, seethed and waited for Jesus to come to her. No longer would she sit at his feet.

But, Martha, at the approach of Jesus and his disciples, immediately broke the bounds of her previous civility and left the mourning women and ran to meet Jesus. The struggle of caring for her brother and living in the crucible of her family's and community's anger and lack of appreciation had made her aware of the strength and power which she knew has not come from her. We simply do not know what happened to her. Something got hold of this woman of tradition and convention who had expressed herself previously only in actions. Now she ran to the Lord and sang a psalm of moaning which had as its melody assurances of God's steadfast love.

Lord it you would have been here, my brother would not have died
But, even now if you ask God, God will give it to you!

John 11:22-23

This was not bargaining, not begging. On the contrary, this was a faithful woman taking to Jesus assured of God's power. When one sees death and beholds sickness, it will clarify things beyond life. Martha requested on this day what she sent word to Jesus of Lazarus illness – that Jesus heal him. She is the first person in the Bible to understand that resurrection comes because of Jesus. Resurrection does not rest upon the fact that God has the power to resurrect human beings, but that Jesus wants us resurrected. The belief that death is not the end is guarded by our friendship with Christ, not out belief in God. Resurrection does not rest upon the fact that God has the power to resurrect humanity, but that Jesus wants us resurrected. The belief that death is not the end is guarded by our friendship with Jesus, not our belief in God. Martha was a different woman than the one Jesus had left a few days before. On this day, this silent woman held a theological conversation with the Lord.

But one other sister remained. Where was Mary? Still sitting in the house of mourning, she was still frozen in her emotions of pain, anger and embarrassment. Martha went back to the house and did something quite extraordinary. She told her sister that Jesus had asked for her. This she did even though there was no mention of this request in the biblical text. Martha reached out to her hurting sister and gave her permission to run toward Jesus, but Jesus did not have to come to her. She knew that Mary was hurting. Before her brother's death, she had requested that Mary leave the presence of Jesus in order to help her with the household chores, but now she wanted her sister to run to his presence.

For whatever reason, it is not uncommon for the one sibling, disgusted by another sibling's unrelenting self-assured faith, to wish that something would happen in order to shake that faith. This does not stem from some malicious intent. Rather, sometimes someone who is important to you can become so consumed by intimacy with God that he or she can have little time for intimacy with others. The feeling is, literally, faith in God has stolen a loved one away. The wish is that something would moderate the force of their convictions and make room for us.

Yet, when sickness, disease and death dislodge another's faith, it is a horrible sight. Worse than not believing is to have believed and lost faith. Martha knew that Mary needed the kind of faith that her sister previously held. Somewhere during the sickness of her brother, Martha had lost all resentment and/or envy of her sister's relationship with Jesus. Now Martha understood what Jesus was attempting to tell her when she objected to her sister's sitting at his feet. Her sister needed a different kind of relationship with Jesus than did Martha. Mary needed a different healing than Martha could have given her. Martha bore the pain of knowing that she didn't have what her sister needed. She had no explanation. Her conversation with Jesus had met her needs but not her sister's. Martha instinctively knew that Mary needed her own experience with Jesus.

So Martha found it in her heart to whisper to her sister: "The master calls for you." Mary rose and ran to meet him. Her sister's support had given her what she could not find in himself – a reason to rise.

When Martha spoke these words to her sister, Mary's feet took on the wings of desperation. She ran! Mary ran with such force and desperation that those who mourned with her were sure that she had been overwhelmed with grief and was headed to the grave of her brother. But she was not running to the grave. Little did she know, she was running toward the resurrection. She was running to her beloved Jesus who had come back for her. Martha's journey into sickness had brought her a freedom of expression and an understanding of Jesus as the Messiah. When she ran to Jesus, she affirmed her faith and discovered a belief. Mary's flight was in hopes of reclamation of a relationship.

Her flight to Jesus was for an explanation. She was going to rekindle an old relationship. Therefore, when she got to him, at the very slight of him she just fell and wept. Through the sobs she said, "If you had been here my brother would not have died." Martha moaned with faith but Mary only wept with regret and pain. Martha had engaged Jesus on matters of death and resurrection. She had assured him that now she believed that Jesus had to be the One. But, Mary, she just wanted to know one thing: Where was Jesus when she needed him?

Mary's hurt was not selfish, it was however, personal. In her weeping and sobbing, she just wanted the Lord to know how she felt. She did not ask him a question. She didn't mean any harm, but she just wanted him to know that friends don't treat other friends like this. She wanted him to know that she waited and believed in him and he let her down. That's weeping – a flood of unrestrained emotions without polish or posturing. That's what people of faith want to do when sickness or disease have taken their loved ones. This weeping is what we are afraid to do. That's why she froze when she heard Jesus was in Bethany. She could not trust herself to lose all composure and risk hearing the silence of a God who would not, or could not, answer her.

Mary's weeping had brought the weeping of others. Jesus was surrounded by weeping. The mourners had followed Jesus and wept with Mary. Jesus was in the presence of uncontrollable grief and he was affected – Jesus wept. It was obvious that he had not come back to Bethany to weep and moan with Mary and Martha. In fact, he never got to their house. The scriptures recount that their time between his notification of Lazarus' sickness and his arrival in Bethany is filled with a discussion between Jesus and His disciples in which they could not believe his seemingly cold detachment concerning the situation in Bethany. Jesus even said to his disciples that Lazarus would only sleep. Whatever interpretation one wants to place on this text, it is clear

Jesus had not anticipated the effect that this grief was going to have on him.

Jesus wept and when Jesus wept, we as Christians believe that God cried. Jesus wept, not over the biological death of Lazarus; he wept over the impact that the hurt and pain of death represented to his friends. If Jesus knew that Lazarus was going to be resurrected later, then there was no reason to weep. God has no reason to weep over our death, but our friends can't help but weep. They have another reason to weep. They love us. John placed in the mouth of a bystander an observation about Jesus at the grave of Lazarus, "Behold he loved him!" (John 11:36)

Out of love, Jesus wept and called for the grave to be opened. He was oblivious to the conversation about his power or his prestige. If he heard the crowd murmuring, asking why Jesus had not healed his friend, he did not address them. The questions of why people suffer and why they must die have never really engaged God. They have been left largely unanswered. In the book of Job, the Lord basically concluded that we don't know enough to either ask the question about suffering or understand the answer if God were to give it to us. But Mary's implicit questions - "Do you care?" ,"Are you my friend?"," What kind of friend are you anyway?" only addressed to a God who asks for love from humanity. God cannot resist moaning and mourning. If these questions come from friends, they ultimately must be answered, or no friendship can exist. An answer is not necessarily an explanation, but a self-revelation.

So when Jesus asked for the grave to be opened, Martha told him that the body had already begun to decompose. She did not understand. Jesus had to reveal something about himself to Martha for her healing. Jesus' reply was only that he had to show her the glory of God. She must see that God is trustworthy. She must behold that life is not in vain and that suffering does end. For Martha, an explanation was enough, but for Mary, Jesus had to answer the questions of friendship and answer the emotions of grief, which surrounded him. He had taken the risk of coming to humanity, and he knew what we needed most of all; if not an explanation from God, at least a revelation that we can trust that we mean something special to God. We need to know that our crying is not in vain, that our trusting is not a cruel joke, and that all our praying is something other than a neat psychological tool to get us through a crisis. We need a mustard seed of faith to move our mountain of doubt in the time of our hurt.

This is what Jesus understood, and curiously the writer John said that Jesus had to pray to God. Yes, this is the characteristic of John to make us aware of Jesus communication with God (John 17). However, in this instance, this conversation is a purposeful inclusion in order to clarify the point that this resurrection was not about a divine plan, but it was about an assurance to those who grieve. It is written that Jesus prayed, "Because of the people who stand by, I said it, that they may believe that you have sent me."

Martha discovered that Jesus could demand, on the basis of his friendship with us, that we be resurrected. Because Jesus knows how much it hurts to lose a loved one and see the suffering, Mary found out that Jesus would demand that they and we be resurrected. In order for us to trust the presence of Jesus, even when we can't understand God's ways, we are given this assurance – death is not eternal and suffering does end for Jesus friends. Mary's relationship was restored. Her relationship with the Lord was not irrelevant. If her prayers could not stop Lazarus from dying and her vigil for Jesus could not hasten his coming, but her faith was not in vain. Jesus continued to have meaning and presence beyond the grave.

Mary's crying and Martha's weeping has resonance for those who have to deal with the death of loved ones. For some, the ordeal with sickness, suffering and death have convinced us that life is too short to be constrained to the roles that everyone else has prescribed for us. We have been left with a more mature and resolute understanding of the sovereignty, power and grace of God. In either case, we are not the same, and our understanding of God is not the same.

Ultimately, we have learned what Mary, Martha and perhaps even Jesus learned: that the mourning and moaning at the grave of a friend can deepen and broaden our confidence in the friend's resurrection. For the sake of our friendship with the Lord, we can be assured that weeping and wailing endure for a season, but joy comes in the morning. We shall rise again. Behold! God hears us. God weeps with us, and Jesus will not endure an eternal separation from his friends. We have an advocate with God who pleads our case and contends for the resurrection of his friends. It is into the hands of this weeping Jesus, standing at the grave of his friend, that we leave our loved ones. We know that our friend will not let us down. Lazarus rose, and we know that our brothers, sisters, wives, husbands, grand parents, friends and loved ones shall rise again.

Questions and Exercises for Discussion

1. Read I Corinthians 15:20-58. Discuss the assurance of the resurrection is discussed in the previous chapter

2. In this chapter two types of mourners were described and embodied in Mary and Martha. Because there are Marys and Marthas in your community or congregation, discuss the differing pastoral responses to each of these mourners. (How does one help Marry rise? How does one help Martha answer her questions?)

3. Sometimes sickness can fracture a family along the lines of personality differences that are judged as differences of love. Has any participate in your group experience this? Invite them to share about the ways in which they healed these rifts.

4. "Not *forgiving* is like drinking poison and expecting the other person to die." (Unknown) Therefore if the poison of non-forgiveness has entered your family through sickness it is time to ask yourself: Is it time to let it go? Have members of your group play the role of Mary or Martha having a conversation about forgiving one another. Then, if you have to do so, go forth and practice this in your family. It is not hurting others but it is infecting you!

The World of the Spirit

*So far then we have seen that, through our Lord Jesus Christ, by faith
we are judged righteousness and at peace with God.
(Romans 5:1)(Jerusalem Bible)*

*Now therefore, there is no condemnation to them that are in Christ
Jesus, who walk not after the Spirit.
(Romans 8:1)(Schofield Bible)*

It is clear, regardless of the pronouncement of preachers and health
care professionals and our better judgments, that we human beings
cannot resist the seduction of blame or its hideous sibling – guilt.
Perhaps this is due to a massive failure of our imaginations. Do you
suppose it is simply an outgrowth of our collective ego's refusal to
accept the existence of a world, which operates outside our influence?
Whatever the reason, guilt and blame assert control over our every
thought and influence our every relationship. They intrude upon our
mental and physical health. They are the allies of sickness and
disease.

We cannot imagine a world free of guilt and blame. What could we do
with our legitimate feelings of regret and remorse? How would we
come face to face with the bad choices that we've made? Perhaps
what is most pressing is that, without the comfort of blaming oneself, or
without judging others, we could neither face those whom we love nor
resist being torn apart by those whom we think hate us. Indeed,
humans have come to rely upon blame and guilt for both passion and
disgust. What is unknown (and therefore feared) and labeled as
impossible is a world of forgiveness and redemption. This is the world
described in this part of the first century A.D. It is a world not after the
flesh but after the spirit.

Perhaps the Roman church already knew such a world. Although Paul
had not visited this church and probably did not know those who
established it, it had survived an edict of expulsion from the Emperor
Claudius and consisted of many different personalities who sought the
same world. Paul knew that they would want to know what kind of
world he envisioned. Therefore, this letter was not about the miracles of
Jesus, but about the miracle of Christ, who is the salvation of the world
and those in it.

Every Christian knows that the label he or she wears, Christian, is less telling than is first presumed. The strange democracy of the church is confusing. Some who have accepted Christ still linger under the seductive spell of guilt and blame. For this reason they consider themselves, on the one hand, superior and holier than thou, and on the other, inferior, always confessing their sins. Such Christians act out their inferiority and superiority complexes in the luster of the Divine. They cannot be comfortable in their own humanity or in the humanity of those around them. To always feel the burden of one's own "sins" and to be disgusted by the "sins" of the others is a miserable, closed existence.

Such feelings and beliefs are especially destructive, violent and painful in the time of sickness and disease. The battles of life and death in one's body often invade the furtive fields of mind and spirit. At such a time, the world's blame and guilt resound with the blame and guilt within us. Did I cause this? Why couldn't I have lived differently? Why didn't I listen to others? Maybe I deserve this? These are the questions that rage in the minds of all human beings who face mortality and stare into the face of predicted death and wasting away. Unfortunately, our technology and medical sophistication, which is perceived as ascribing more causes and effects to human behavior than is its intention, seems only to reinforce these destructive calls within us. For Christians to not offer the powers of faith, forgiveness, and grace to themselves or someone else suffering in such a battle is to deny the very presence of God or, in the case of Christians, Christ.

Paul's letter to the Roman Church begins by lamenting the world of the flesh, which has no redemption and no Christ. He etches a terrifying etching of the landscape of loneliness, guilt and universal condemnation. The Law, a system of right and wrong and rules and regulations, seemed to be against human existence. God is reduced to nothing more than a police officer or judicial figure constrained to mandatory sentencing of the non-religious. Everybody is guilty of something. Even those who claim to be holy and faithful get condemned for their sins. None can escape:

What then? Are we better than they? No, in no way, for we have before proved both Jews and Greeks that they are all under sin. As it is written: there is none righteous, no not one… All have sinned and come short of the glory of God. (Romans 3: 9-12; 3:23)

In this world, before Christ, none are free. All are equal prisoners. Paul recognizes that people's actions can be and are destructive to themselves and to those around them. He does not deny that physical actions do possess consequence. Which of us have not mourned lost opportunities? Who among us does not have a life filled with some regrets? A broken relationship, children who reject us, jail sentences, jobs that have been lost, heart attacks striking those of us who are overweight, the unclean needles and sex without condoms. All of these are undeniable evidence of the consequential nature of the world of the flesh. A world whose unrelenting law is immutable: For every action there is an equal and opposite reaction (Newton's first law of physics).

As quiet as it is kept, before the eyes of God, Christians do not claim physical differentiation from others. We are still subject to the consequences of the laws of the flesh. In the assignment of blame, guilt, and shame, were equally deserving. There are no good people, nor bad people. There is no sin, which is worse than any other sin. This is the crux of the Pauline and Christian arguments: left to a cold, hard application of the Law, every one of us ought to be dead and/or suffering. All of us have hurt people for no reason, have habits that destroy our bodies, have made choices that should have gotten us killed, and thrown enough financial opportunities away to deserve poverty. According to the world of the flesh, all is us deserve the plight of those who are suffering and dying.

However, if anyone joins the chorus of blame and shame, it should only those who live in the world of the flesh, a world devoid of Christ. Arrogance and superiority have no place in the world of the Spirit. Those who would argue as to which sins are not abominations before God do not walk after the spirit. Such people have always infected the church. They simply cannot give up the comfort of feeling better than someone else. But Paul speaks directly to those who condemn others. "If you indeed knew as much, then you are twice as guilty as those whom you are condemning. You not only show no compassion, but you have the audacity to judge someone else who is equally as guilty as you" (Romans 2: 1-3). In the time of sickness and disease, this aspect of the world of the flesh is most galling and appalling. Redemption is surely needed by all.

Without the dawn of God's forgiveness, what is most frightening about this dark landscape through the saving act of Jesus Christ, is that there are no rays of hope or justice. There is no active independent God. From the end of the third chapter until the sixth chapter of Romans, Paul paints another picture for us Christians, one vibrant with the crimson blood of a redemptive suffering. It is, after all, God who initiates the world of the Spirit. From the beginning of the world, through the sacred stories of Abraham and Sarah and David and the wife of Uriah, the Deity constantly strains to direct the world to a more excellent way. God seduces humanity by love of justice and the free gift of faith to let go of blame and guilt and turn our faces to the things of the spirit-forgiveness, grace and acceptance. Paul writes:

Apply this to Abraham, the ancestor from whom we are all descended. If Abraham was justified as a reward for doing something, he would really have something to boast about; Abraham put his faith in God's sight, because scripture says: Abraham put his faith in God and this faith was considered as justifying him. If a man has work to show, his wages are not considered as a favor but as his due; but when a man has nothing to show except faith in the one who justifies sinners, then his faith is considered as justifying him. And David says then: a man is happy if God considers him righteous, irrespective of his good deeds. Happy are those whose crimes are forgiven, whose sins are blotted out; happy is the man whom the Lord considers sinless.
(Romans 4: 1-8)

Yet, we fight our own salvation. We resist life. We suspect it and time and time again, we deny its healing power. Bitterness and blaming for hurts, which will not heal, keep us from accepting this love. We want consequences.

As odd as it sounds, we want consequences because they explain things. If it were true that only IV drug users or homosexuals get AIDS, then as an IV drug user or a gay person I could at least explain the reasons for the horrors I am facing. By quietly rejecting the love of the ones around me, I could feel as if I were atoning for my sins, alternatively by presuming that people who seem to care for me now are only fulfilling their own need to pity. I could lash out and make them pay for their earlier rejection of me. As a non-IV drug user or a heterosexual person I could pretend that AIDS really does follow an order of the physical universe and that people are dying as a consequence of the way they lived their lives. But the little comfort it might give, in terms of explaining the horror, is at a cost too dear.

As an IV drug user or a homosexual person who revels in self-blame, such blame destroys my ability to experience the healing and grace of genuine love, whether from loved ones who previously rejected me or from strangers who made the world a little less. As a non-IV drug user or heterosexual person, the guilt of someone infected with AIDS may only give me a false sense of security that can kill me if it lulled me into having unprotected and/or casual sex. It may also rob me of opportunities to show compassion, and thus be enriched by the lives of those infected persons whom God fills with grace and courage.

To blame the victim, who is the real definition of a consequential world, brings order and reason to a situation. However, it brings it at the price of mercy. No sexual orientation, lifestyle, addiction or circumstance should sentence one to death or deny one the right to experience and give love. For this reason, that no one is deemed worthy of death and suffering, Jesus died. Paul wrote:

So then we have seen that, through our Lord Jesus Christ, by faith was judged righteous and at peace with God.
Romans 5:1

Paul contends that the death, burial and resurrection of Jesus forever banishes the world of the flesh and calls us to a world of peace with God and one another. This is the good news. This is the world of the Spirit that beckons to all who profess to be Christians.

Unfortunately, even after God initiates such a world, human beings have great difficulty in trusting in its existence. To do so would involve making oneself vulnerable. It also means expecting love, justice and forgiveness from people. Even the most faithful among us do not easily enter such a world. We may not believe that people are as good as we, but experience has confirmed that people are at least as bad as we.

This world of the Spirit seems such a fantasy. It seems to be built for humans unlike ourselves. Therefore, we do not trust it. Given this human characteristic of distrust, the world of the Spirit will be nothing but a good thought. It will never be real. But we will never be able to believe in the power of the world of the Spirit if we do not first enter this world ourselves. To convince one of the powers of the Spirit is to live by the Spirit. Paul wrote of the experience of living in the world of the Spirit while existing in the world of the flesh.

In fact, this seems to be the rule, that every single time I want to do good, it is something else that comes to hand. In my inmost self I dearly love God's Law, but I can see that my body follows a different law, which my reason dictates. The reason, therefore, why those who are in Christ Jesus are not condemned, is that the law of the Spirit of life in Christ Jesus has set you free from the law of sin and death. God has done what the Law, because of our unspiritual nature, was unable

to do. God dealt with sin by sending his own Son in a body as physical as any sinful body, and in that body God condemned sin. God did this in order that the Law just demands might be satisfied in us, who behave not as our spiritual nature but as the spirit dictates.
Romans 7:21-23; 8:1-4)

Christ Jesus has set you free! The world of the Spirit involves the acceptance of this freedom. Guilt, judgment, shame and blame are chains that bind our hearts and minds. They keep old wounds fresh. These chains all come from a sense that we are somehow responsible for all that goes wrong in our lives. Thus, in a fit of frustration and pain, we often make bad situations worse. Paradoxically, all the successful programs for treating alcoholics' addiction have discovered that one of the essential steps to recovery in not taking control over one's own world. Rather, it is the acceptance of a higher power. One takes responsibility for one's own actions, but not blame for their outcomes. In other words, the past becomes an ally and teacher, not shameful burden. The uncertain future becomes an inspiration for action, not guilt-ridden excuse for fearful apathy.

Not until we unburden ourselves, by loving all that we are, can we enter the world of the Spirit. The total package of past, present and future deserves no condemnation. We are all beautiful, God has accepted us all. We have entered the dwelling place of God. God is present with us in our experience of the life of the Spirit while we exist in the "Law" of the flesh. We then can accept others in the presence of the forgiveness of God, which is to forget blame. In the world of the Spirit life is "for-giving" and "for-getting" away from the chains of the past. It is "for-giving" love to ones closest to us and "for-getting" away from the accusation of what was said. Life is "for-giving" ourselves a chance to love us and "for-getting" away from the idea that we do not deserve love. In the world of the spirit life is "for-giving" to others and "for-getting" away from an accounting of what others have taken away from us. It is in this world that God is present.

Paul goes on to other matters. But for us the words at the end of the eighth chapter of Romans are enough for our struggle with death, dying, suffering, living and loving in the world of the Spirit.

After saying this, what can we add? With God on our side, who can be against us? Since God did not spare God's own Son, but gave him up to benefit us all, we may be certain, after such a gift, that we will not refuse anything God can give. Could anyone accuse those whom God has condemned? Could Jesus Christ? No! He not only died for us—he rose from the dead, and there at God's right hand he stands and pleads for us.

(Romans 3: 1-34)

Question and Exercise for Discussion

Read the eighth chapter of the book of Romans, and based upon this reading and this study, do the following exercise and answer the following questions.

1. How have blame and guilt infected and affected your life?

2. In what ways have blame and guilt influenced and affected the church? How has this infection affected your thoughts and attitudes about the church, specifically, and people of faith in general?

3. Take a piece of paper and divide it into three columns. Over one column, label regrets. Over another, label reasons for the regrets. Finally, over a third column, label God's action and mine. Now list the regrets in your life that you have. Take your time to list them. Then fill up the second column with the reasons for your regrets. Now write in large bold letters across the first and second column, "Forgiven and Forgotten by God."

4. What are the wrong messages that the church has given to people? List the ones that have hurt you or someone you know. Are they based on scriptures? Are they based on personal prejudice? If you are doing this in a group, share your list. After you or your group have come to an agreement on these messages, discuss when the most destructive ones come from and how we can change them.

5. Blame and guilt are sinister things that can steal out basic ability to love ourselves and the people around us. So the following is an exercise that is intended to allow us to recover that which these two thieves may have taken. Do you love yourself? Why not? In the world of the Spirit, God not only loves you but also allows you to love all that you are. If you are doing this exercise with a family member or loved one, list five wonderful things about each other that you love and share them.

Going Through the Roof
For The Sake of a Friend

*Some men appeared carrying on a bed a paralyzed
man whom they were trying to bring in and lay down
in front of him. But as the crowd made it impossible to
find a way of getting him in, they went up on the flat
roof and lowered him and his stretcher down through
the tiles into the middle of the gathering, in front of
Jesus. Seeing their faith he said, "My friend, your sins
are forgiven."*

*The Scribes and Pharisees began to think this over.
"Who is this man talking blasphemy? Who can forgive
sins but God alone?" But Jesus, aware of their
thoughts, made them this reply: "What are these
thoughts you have in your hearts? Which of these is
easier to say' Your sins are forgiven you or to say,' Get
up and walk?' But to prove to you that the Son of Man
has authority on earth to forgive sins,"- he said to the
paralyzed man- "I order you: get up, and pick up your
stretcher and go home." And immediately before their
very eyes he got up. Picked up what he had been lying
on and went home praising God.*

Luke 5: 17 – 25

They are more refreshing than a cool rain in a hot, muggy July. They
are more surprising than a thunderbolt from a clear blue sky. They are
more precious than all the precious jewels in the earth. They give us
the gifts of laughter and mirth. They are not natural nor are they
manufactured. Surely, they must come from God. They are—our friends.

For no reason and for many reasons our friends both affirm and create
our faith in our fellow human beings. They make a huge world smaller,
more intimate and more manageable. Unlike family in which one is
born, friends can simply walk away with little or no shame. They have
no ironclad obligations to bind them to us, just the integrity of their
promises. Their existence in our lives is so incredible that we constantly
guard against believing in these rather strange relationships.

We use the label "friend" often, but because we realize that these
relationships can be as treacherous as falling in love, we do not let our

hearts believe the label but for a few. We count our "true" friends with stingy pride. Constantly they are tested as to the strength of their commitment to us. We hope to share our most intimate physical and emotional self with our best friend. Beyond that one, who becomes bound to us by obligation and promise, most of us believe that these special people are few indeed. Besides our families, it is their smiles, tears, laughter, silliness and seriousness that fill the treasure boxes of our memories. If there is one gift that sickness and disease offer, it is the discovery that there are many more friends in our lives than we suspected. From the horizontal position of a sick bed one often encounters the face of God in the faces of one's friends.

The hour of need offers to those who are healthy a precious gift of giving. Just as we seek confirmation of our friends true commitments, we yearn for ways to express our gratitude for what friends have meant to our world. Sentiment and words seem awkward, and gifts and symbols never seem adequate. In fact, one never escapes the feeling that something ought to be said. Sickness gives us the opportunity to demonstrate our care. Nothing is more difficult than to have a friend in need and not be able to help him or her.

This is the situation with the friends of the paralytic man. They were filled with futility. Their friend is paralyzed. No other condition is so devastating. It means that the man is excruciatingly vulnerable. There are no modern technological tools to assure his independence. The paralytic man is totally at the mercy and goodwill of the others around him. His body had become his prison and the people around him could either be his wardens or his friends. Health is the measure of one's freedom and he has lost every bit of freedom that he had. He cannot even physically get to Jesus. It appears that he is utterly without hope.

His horror story is what most of us dread. None of us ever want it said of us that we are "on someone's hands" or a burden to the lives of our loved ones and friends. Whether these characterizations are true or not, they nonetheless describe the horror that we imagine. We fear the possible transformation of our relationships of love, promise and mutual obligations to ones of duty and mercy alone. In such a state we suppose that the kindness and generosity of friends many become difficult to accept. That which is most necessary for a good friendship– mutual giving–would be destroyed. A friend would become just another health care professional. He or she would come to know the most intimate details of our lives, not out of choice but out of necessity. Such a situation can destroy friendships.

Worse yet, we fear that our friend would become weary of us and abandon us. We imagine that their goodwill has a limit. Our nightmare is that we will have to accept their departure without so much as a protest because we will understand their leaving. Time and time again we would have to relive that deep sense of hurt, betrayal, and loss that only a friend can cause. We are scared of a world without friends to make life livable and laughable. The plight of a paralytic man represents the greatest test of the strength and integrity of friendships.

This Bible story is a testament to friends. It is so stunning that is a part of the synoptic gospels (Matthew 9:2-8, Mark 2:1-12 and Luke 5:18 - 26) In varying degrees of detail, every gospel writer pays tribute to the men who carried the paralyzed man to Jesus. Each synoptic gospel writer adapts the telling of this story in order to illuminate major themes in his own gospel. In none of these stories is the man allowed to speak. Jesus does not seek after the man. Rather, the paralytic man is thrust into the world of healing by his friends. It is clear that the religious authorities have problems with the healing, and it is the faith of the man's friends that He commends before he heals him.

These friends of the paralytic man refused to be bystanders in their friend's life. They refused to be supporting actors in the nightmare of dependency. Sickness has many allies in its efforts to destroy human beings. Financially, it has poverty. Spiritually, it has shame and blame. Socially, it has solitude and loneliness. These elements when combine together in someone's life, sickness can reduce life to a veritable hell on earth.

Healing also had allies. Healing is not a passive process. It is a battle against the influences of death. Friends are the major foot soldiers against sickness and disease. They can attack loneliness by their mere presence and cause shame to flee by a hug. They can destroy blame with an arsenal of affirmation and information. Friends can prop up hope and give aid to perseverance. They can even help remove the victory from death with a celebration of life.

However, In order to aid in the process of healing, friends must first overcome the attacks of hopelessness and futility which sickness visits upon them. Before this paralytic man's friends could get him in the presence of the Healer, they had to overcome the obstacles of the people around the Healer. It was not uncommon in that time period or geographic location for people to call themselves healers, Or to claim that they had a gift of healing. It can be safely assumed that the friends of the paralytic must have carried him to the other healers. Each time they thought, "This healer will be the one." Each time they were thrust into a greater sense of hopelessness. Anyone who has gone through the ups and downs of innovative drugs, radiation therapy, chemotherapy, remission and the good and bad days of a chronically ill person knows about the sense of anticipation and disappointment that go along with the pursuit of hope.

With each failed attempt at healing, the man's disappointment must have become greater. But friends are constrained to not show disappointment. They must attempt to mourn a loss of hope without officiating over the death of hope. Friends worry most about doing and saying the "right" things. One doesn't want to encourage fantasies but one also doesn't want to suppress faith. One doesn't want to speak too much of the future to someone who may not have a future, but one who wants a suffering friend to somehow live beyond his or her painful present. You may find yourself praying with a friend for miracles of medicine and faith while encouraging the creation of Living Wills and Durable Powers of Attorneys. Friends find themselves in extended conversations about resurrection as much as about healing.

Each failure must have been more and more difficult on the friends of the paralytic man. Perhaps this is why the people around Jesus were so unwilling to let him get to Jesus. The crowds had let him pass so many other times. They had become hardened to the sight of the paralytic man being carried on the shoulders of his friends. The longer his condition lasted, the more his friends shared the man's sense of solitude. They also shared his anger at being forgotten.

Therefore, out of desperation or anger, the difficulty of the crowd's refusal only made them more determined that their friend would have a chance at healing. They had become his advocates with others and God. Theirs was a prayer of action. Whether he wanted to go before God or not, they would place him there. Such perseverance is always encouraged in scripture. People are always told to pray for others. They are always told that their prayers matter. They are never told to give up. Only the tormentors of Job, the extreme examples of bad friends, could advise their friend to give up on hope. Every hope, within reason and grasp, had to be given to their friend.

So they climbed to the roof and literally tore it apart to get to the Healer. Clearly, this was uncouth and disruptive, but it was their job to do what he could not do. It is the nature of advocacy; when for whatever reason your friend is locked out of the presence of his or her healing; you demand his or her right to treatment and care, even if it means stepping out of the bond of civility. People who have campaigned for orphan drugs, wider distribution of experiential drugs and who have done war with the bigots in their church who will not offer the gifts of acceptance and hope to their friends are all inheritors of "going through the roof for the sake of a friend."

Perhaps this is why this story was written. Could it be that the actions of these men who bore this man on his cart were actually the will of God? Could that kind of loyalty and advocacy for the sick and suffering be an integral part of the passion of this narrative of Jesus and subsequently the church? Incredibly, Jesus himself answered "yes"." When he looked at the man who had been lowered from the roof a curious thing happened. In all the account in all three gospels, Jesus said; "Because of so great a faith, your sins are forgiven." Whose faith? The man is only mentioned as the object of his friends' faith. The only subjects in the story were his friends. The faith of his friends had moved the Healer. Jesus must have glanced up from the paralytic man's condition of suffering and fixed his stare on their faces of hope and faith when he uttered these words. Only after his argument with the Pharisees and Scribes do the scriptures expressly state that Jesus turned to the man and ordered him to take up his bed and walk." Jesus honored the faith of his friends.

His friends were not powerless. They had many gifts to offer their friend. They were the principals in this healing story. Their prayers of action and their persistence in faith were absolutely necessary to this healing. They were necessary then as they are today to the healing stories of those who are sick today. Friends have a ministry. They also have a message to those who surround Jesus: Sometimes you have to "go through the roof for the sake of a friend."

Questions and Exercises for Discussion

1. Read Job, chapters 11 and 14, and compare the kind of friendship Job's friends displayed and the friendship that the friends of the paralytic man displayed. What are the characteristics of a good friend and a bad friend?

2. Share stories of how friends have built up your faith or how they have torn it down.

3. How is your church and/or community been a friend or an advocate to those who are sick? Are there those among you that need somebody to "go through the roof" for them? Look around and see who may be being denied treatment because of finances or forms they cannot understand or, worse yet, who may be being denied the comfort of the church.

When a "No" Just Won't Do

*He (Jesus) left that place and set out for the
territory of Tyre. There he went into a house
and did not want anyone to know he was there
but he could not pass unrecognized.*

*A woman whose little daughter had an unclean
spirit heard about him straightway and came
and fell at his feet. Now the woman was a
pagan, by birth a Syrophenician, and she
begged him to cast the devil out of her
daughter. And he said to her, "The children
should be fed first, because it is not fair to take
the children's food and throw it to the house
dogs."
But she spoke up: "Ah, yes,sir," she replied,
"but the house dogs under the table can eat
the children's scrapes." And he said to her,
"For saying this, you may go home happy: the
devil has gone out of your daughter." So she
went off to her home and found the child lying
on the bed and the devil gone.
Mark 7:24-30 see also Matt 15: 21-28*

Name-calling can be ignored. Insults can be endured. Having to stay in your place can be tolerated. These are the rules under which a segregated society operates. For better or worse people tend to stay in their own communities. But when segregation becomes an obvious matter of life and death, the excluded will be silenced or shunned. They will not accept death by prejudice and discrimination. The rules must be broken. The status quo must go. Out of sheer need, a revolutionary is born and a protest is begun. Such a moment came to a Syrophenician woman when her child was possessed of an evil spirit and she heard that Jesus, the Healer. was in the area.

No one really knows why Jesus went to Tyre. Mark simply wrote that he wished "to be hidden." Explanations of his action ranged from a simple desire for rest to a theory that Mark included this stroll through Tyre and Sidon in order to demonstrate to the early Christian community that Jesus did, indeed, intend to bring the Gospel to the Gentiles.

Whatever the reasons, Jesus surely could not be hidden. Anyone who claims to be a messenger of hope, healing and love cannot choose when, where or who will be attracted to these messages. Every human being assumes that he or she deserves these gifts from God. Confessions such as these invite testing and guarantee an audience. In fact, it would be particularly mean to proclaim the presence of hope, healing and love, but deny these to some and freely give them to others.

Even though she was a Syrophoenician, the witness of Jesus persuaded her that she could approach him. Jesus and those who followed him had become well known for doing unusual miracles. They were rumored to be unlike those whom she despised and feared. Still, had it not been for her great need, she may not have gone. She would have stayed in her place. Despite all that she heard about Jesus, she was not drawn to him. Rather, her need was such that she could not ignore him. A desperate search for hope brought her to Jesus. The love for her daughter and her frustration concerning a seemingly incurable condition were her evangelists.

The presence of sickness, disease and spiritual crisis in one's life may cause a human being to seek out those who have been previously ignored or considered ridiculous. Because futility is as incomprehensible as hope, one becomes open to the possibility of a healing from a source that cannot be explained. All of her reasons and thoughts, of course, cannot understand. They are as unknown as the reasons for Jesus' presence in Tyre. Perhaps Mark is wise to leave such matters unresolved. Nonetheless, it simply must be noted that it took an odd mixture of courage, desperation and faith to bring her to Jesus.

Imagine her hurt when she came to him and Jesus and his disciples confirmed all of her worst fears. Jesus not only seemed to rebuke her request for the healing of her daughter, but he did so with a radical slur. Fully cognizant of her needs and looking at her desperation, Jesus did a cruel, brutal and unsavory deed. He refused her simple request. Why this woman? He had healed so many others who had not shown her courage or demonstrated her need. In fact, Jesus had previously healed a woman hemorrhaging blood. (Mark 5:21 – 34). He even singled her out and commended her for her extraordinary faith. Was not the syropheonician woman's courage and need for compassion as striking, if not more astonishing, as the woman with the issue of blood?

For anyone who reads this story as a person of faith, this is a most difficult moment. Jesus is downright embarrassing. Commentators have wished to excuse him by noting that in the Greek or Aramaic language his rebuke was not really that mean. They contend that he referred to her as puppy, not dog. Somehow this is supposed to be endearing and playful. Preachers have tried to hide this slip of compassion by either not preaching this text or quickly moving on to the miraculous end of the story. Christians in general have tried to lessen its impact, asking that Jesus be forgiven for this indiscretion because of the pressing need to save the world. None of these lessen the stark reality that Jesus said no in a particularly hurtful manner and Mark had the boldness to write it into scripture.

The haunting image of this story is that Jesus as the Son of God, and Jesus as the son of humanity, could be so close to someone's needs and yet seem so far away. Because God chooses to be involved in human experience in order to transform this world, sometimes the meanness and ugliness of the world can make it very hard indeed to approach God. A tendency to discriminate infects all humanity. Any deity who chooses to become enrobed in flesh will be exposed to the diseases of the flesh, not sins but diseases. A sense of tribalism and identification with a culture are the inevitable outgrowth of physical existence. Everyone has "his or her people". Relationships define loyalties. Jesus' rebuke did not arise out of his identity, an oppressed second century Palestinian Jew, as much as it arose out of his humanity. It is the struggle of every faith and religious community to rid himself or herself of this disease.

In fact, faith is supposedly one of the few bridges that can reach between differing peoples, yet communities of faith have often produced the language and means of exclusion. Discrimination is a human tendency, but the passion of prejudice is often the deformed child of a deeply held faith traditions.

It is this very issue that kept the woman away from Jesus in the first place. Jesus was not a Syrophoenician, and her people had suffered at the hands of his people. Further, Jesus was a religious leader of her enemy. She was a woman, and experience had taught her that she was not valued in religious places. Indeed, hers is the only story in the entire Bible in which a woman asks for the healing of her daughter. It is one of the very few instances in which any woman had asked for the healing of another female. She had every reason to suspect that his compassion would run out when she needed it.

That human being discriminate is unavoidable, but that they assign resources on the basis of their prejudices is dangerous and unacceptable. That is what creates injustice and inequality. The color of one's skin, the amount of one's financial resources, the gender and shape of one's body, the nature of one's culture or one's sexual orientation should not determine whether one lives or dies. It should not determine whether one receives mercy or grace. A pagan woman has as much claim to the blessings of God as any male disciple. The fact that some diseases affect one group of people more than another which is perceived as less desirable for the financial and social well being of a society should not merit a cut in aid to those who suffer. The mere fact that those in need may not be of the Christian tribe does not mean a less passionate or timely response is warranted. Some things are a human right. Her battle for the life of her daughter gave this Syrophoenician woman the courage to believe in this simple truth. She knew what she deserved. She was not going to be discouraged by the confirmation of her fears. Jesus told her:

"The children should be fed first, because it is not fair to take the children's food and throw it to the house dogs."

She replied immediately:

"Ah yes, sir but the house dogs under the table can eat the children's scraps."

As with most cases of Jesus' healing of a woman, this story ultimately turns out to be a monument to her faith, not Jesus' ability to perform miracles. In this story, as well as the woman with the issue of blood or the widow's meager offering, Jesus recognized a simple fact. For any woman to come to Jesus always means getting past the community and traditions surrounding him. Women have mostly populated religious communities around the world, but the majority those in authority of these communities have almost always been men. This form of discrimination and prejudice is oppressive. In Matthew's account of this story, the men demanded that the Syrophoenician woman be sent away with such a silly request. The faith of our fathers has often kept our mothers poor and sick.

The bare fact of the matter is, over the course of time, women have born the brunt of caring for the sick and nurturing the children. While this work is essential for the continuation of any society, it is work which was nonetheless "under- appreciated." In times of sickness and disease, the hands and arms of faith are often feminine. Sometimes women die because they expose themselves so continuously to sickness and disease. Most often, they are simply exhausted by carrying so many lives on their backs, in their hearts and on their minds. The whole time they are doing this, they are subjected to a double standard in the community of faith, which makes it hard to get to Jesus.

This woman knew that she was entitled to an audience with Jesus regardless of what was said to her or how she was treated. She trusted that Jesus was greater than those who surrounded him or the ethnic or religious traditions which bore him. She wrestled with God until God heard her cry and the disciples recognized her faith. For once the story was not about the perseverance of a mother on behalf of her son, but it was about the courage and steadfastness of a woman on behalf of her daughter.

Perhaps this is why Jesus went out of his way to meet this woman. Her story had to be told so that women, who find themselves in need of him, yet find it difficult to tolerate those who surround him, could know that they are not the first to feel skeptical, hurt and rejected. This story is a witness to the fact that although Jesus is a part of a particular tradition, he was not captive to tradition.

Mark and Matthew had to write about the Syrophoenician woman's struggle so that women who have been told by men that there lives are not as valuable as a man's life could have a heroine. This story has to be written so that women who have been socialialized to live in silence in the church could know that they do not have to sit in silence. These gospels had to leave on record that the brutality of indifference or neglect of a woman and her suffering is never the will of Jesus. The story of the Syrophoenician woman had to be written to say, despite the difficulties of the approach to Jesus, there is a healing of women on behalf of women. Sisters can rise up for the sake of sisters and seek their own healing. Mark had to write so it could be clearly noted, in the time of sickness and disease, that religious discrimination and prejudice cannot prevail. We had to know that pagan women who are dying or whose daughters are dying are entitled to the faith, hope and love of Jesus. We had to have a heroine in scripture that was outraged by the possible death of women. It had to be stated- a "No" just won't do!

Questions and Exercises for Discussion

1. Have two people, a man and a woman, read Matthew's version of the stories out loud. The male should read the parts of Jesus and the narrator and the woman should read the part of Jesus. The others in the group should read the part of the disciples. Discuss how it feels to read this passage in gender specific parts. The women in the group should express their feelings and opinions about this passage as the men listen. The men should express their feelings and opinions about this passage as the women listen. Compare and contrast the differences and similarities of these reactions.

2. Prepare a list of health conditions which women are more susceptible than men. Then create a similar list of health conditions for men. Ask which of these has your church responded to and why? Examples are high blood pressure for men and breast cancer for women. Which of these and others on your list is your church most likely to provide information and education?

3. If you are a part of a women's organization in your church, is there more you can do to aid in the healing and health of your sisters? Write down some specifics and share them with other women.

Floyd Thompkins, Jr.

Every Eye that's Shut Ain't Sleep–Every Good-bye Ain't Gone!

Ode to Dr. James Patterson

In Joppa there was a disciple named Tabitha (in Greek her name is Dorcas); she was always doing good and helping the poor. About that time she became sick and died, and her body was washed and placed in an upstairs room. Lydda was near Joppa; so when the disciples heard that Peter was in Lydda, they sent two men to him and urged him, "Please come at once!"
Peter went with them, and when he arrived he was taken upstairs to the room. All the widows stood around him, crying and showing him the robes and other clothing that Dorcas had made while she was still with them.
Peter sent them all out of the room; then he got down on his knees and prayed. Turning toward the dead woman, he said, "Tabitha, get up." She opened her eyes, and seeing Peter she sat up. He took her by the hand and helped her to her feet. Then he called for the believers, especially the widows, and presented her to them alive. This became known all over Joppa, and many people believed in the Lord.
Acts 9: 36-42

For Christians who believe that Christ is a healer one's own death is an answer but to the friends of that a Christian brother or sister who believe similarly, death leaves questions. Why didn't God heal him or her? God, why didn't you, when I have seen the miraculous and the unexplainable for others, heal my friend? Remissions from Cancer, Leukemia, AIDS and other "terminal diagnoses" have left many doctors scratching their heads in wonderment or plain disbelief. In fact some Christians came to their faith after beholding the miraculous in their own lives or the life of another.

The miraculous was the launching point of their faith. For others the miraculous continues to be the ultimate truth that trumps all confusion over facts. The more such events are witnessed and experienced the more they add to a sense of absolute disappointment when someone dies who you believe was a perfect candidate for the miraculous. It just makes God seem more capricious, more inscrutable and more confusing.

60

One hides ones exasperation in an avalanche of platitudes: "The Lord knows best," "They are in a better place," "The healing is not of this world." Whether these sayings are true or not is immaterial. The miracle did not happen for a deserving saint. It should not be so, but the death of a believer makes us mourn as much for the attack on our faith as the absence of our brother or sister. Therefore, it is harder to get over. It is more difficult to let go of the person. One keeps rehearsing the events of our fellow believer's to survive the sickness and experience a miracle in search of a missed step of faith. We call up the memories of all that he or she did for the Lord. We examine the evidence of their good works, their faithful service and their powerful witness and we cannot understand the outcome.

This is the case with the friends of Tabitha or Dorcas. They could not let her go. She was their friend who deserved more from God. The text says, "She was always doing good and helping the poor". In fact, because the text mentioned no husband or children we are lead to the inevitable conclusion that the service to others inhabited her heart to the exclusion of other intimate relationships. She seemed to be self-sacrificing and a pillar of this community.

More than a family was in mourning, a community was in mourning. She was one of those people who seem to be graced with a special ability to transcend the bounds of her particular family and reach into universal human experience. It did not matter whom she resembled, or to whom she was related or where she lived – she just touched everybody. So, everybody mourned her because they knew that something and someone special had touched, enriched and expanded their lives. One does not let such a presence leave you without fighting for it to stay.

We all know people of this ilk and kind. These are people who will not let themselves become defined by their community. They transcend their social, political and religious station in life. It must be said that Dorcas was an unmarried woman. There were multitudes of cultural and religious reasons why her story should not have been told. She should not have been mourned. She should not have been missed. But, some people refuse to be bound by the chains of conventions or prejudice. They refuse to be distracted by insult, ignorance or being ignored. They insist on loving their way into the hearts of people who declare that they do not matter to them.

Floyd Thompkins, Jr.

The labels Black, White, Woman, and Christian, Man, Jewish, Atheist, Straight, Gay, Latino, Handicapped and others are only relevant and intelligible in the context in which they are used.

They are words that are given positive, negative or any meaning at all by agreement with those to whom they are applied and those who utter them. Some among us just won't agree that the label, while defining a historical and cultural context, is in anyway limiting or distinctive. They reach a certainty of their humanity which is both particular in owning the richness of their community with pride and discount the need to defend, discourage or defy any other community, even when it is hostile to them. They find a way to touch everybody.

So these are the people whom you can't tell who they might know. These are the people who forgive the unforgiveable and help any person who is hurting, even though that person would be the last to help him/her. They are people who risk ridicule and rebuke by their own community to help and love someone whom their community deems not deserving of such help. Miraculously, these are people who touch such a broad spectrum of people. They manage to be at the center of everything. Yet, they themselves are not the center of attention.

When these "saints" are attacked by sickness and disease we assume that God will intervene. They, after all, do the work of the Lord more than anyone else. Dorcas in fact, did what she did out of a sense of faith. The text said, "she was a disciple" Her faith was the reason for her courage. Be clear, that it was not just religious faith. She was not described as a religious person. She was a disciple. She put her faith in Jesus! Surely, the follower of a healer would be healed. But, she died in Jappa.

When Dorcas died, the city was shaken. Joppa was a large port city with multitudes but her death caused reverberations, at least among the Christians, in that city. So, profoundly disturbing of an event was it that a city, Lydda, which was located nine miles away heard about it and some mourned there. This unmarried woman demonstrated the power of a loving life and the community was not ready to let her go. Therefore, after she died they sent for Peter. Why? When Dorcas shut her eyes, others were opened. The community saw Dorcas' gift.

When someone like Dorcas is around, we take what they do for granted and we don't appreciate the scope and power of their lives until they're gone. Their funerals and memorial services are times of stunning revelations of their lives. You may find yourself sitting next to

62

someone to whom you would not necessarily talk to on any other occasion. In the recitation of the stories about the life of a Dorcas one finds oneself laughing in unison with people whom one would assume they have nothing in common. The gift of connection is a stunning revelation for those who spend their lives in very particular communities of people like themselves and therefore develop a surprising prejudice based on ignorance.

When Dr. James Patterson was sick I sat with him for the last three weeks of his life, both at his apartment and in the hospital. I was amazed by the diversity of people who came to see him. I knew some of them and I knew that many of them did not know each other. Yet, they were from communities that politically and socially opposed one another in terms of the cultural and political wars at the time. I watched church folk visit him. I saw transgender folk visit him. I saw old folks and young folks visit him. I saw Lesbians and holiness women visit him. I saw extremely wealthy people driven by the chauffeurs visit him. I saw people take the bus and walk up the hill or borrow a car to come visit him. They all had the same experience of coming to say good-bye to their fiend. They all cried inconsolably.

I was called upon to pray with people who did not believe in prayer and travail with people who were certain that prayer worked. We were all different. And I, as a young university chaplain who had known Dr. Patterson for less than a year, became a pastor and a listener of a man struggling with mortality and significance. As his eyes shut, mine opened.

So the widows gathered at Dorcas' house and they brought the clothes. Every life leaves something behind. Memories of those who left us adorn the emotional wardrobes of our lives. We incorporate them in our daily living so that the dead are not gone. So, the widows mourned by holding up the clothes and I suppose telling the stories of how they were made. At Dr. Patterson's home going service we all brought our clothes of life while we wore out physical clothing of mourning. His spirit could not be contained. But, as his pastor and I prepared for the service, we both knew that the question hung in the air. Why?

This time the judgmental presuppositions of sin and disease were not in the majority. Indeed, there were some (there always are) who knew why Dr. Patterson died and why he should not be honored even though they knew nothing. Rather, most of the congregation walked in to look at a man's whose eyes were shut too soon. I anxiously waited to hear what the senior pastor would say. He was a mentor, friend and nationally recognized religious leader. He had experience and wisdom. He said nothing. He didn't even preach. He let the friends of Dr. Patterson speak. He watched the miracle of a life well lived. He knew what Peter knew - Some things are not ours to explain. They are God's to reveal. The message was in the life that was well lived. The explanation was in the gathering.

It is alright to say I don't know. It's okay for Christians to have no defense for God's actions. God will defend and reveal God's self in a way that only the person who asks the question will understand. We don't speak enough emotional languages to satisfy everyone's appetite for an explanation. Peter never said anything to the mourners in the text. They'd sent for him because he was a preacher and a healer. But, when he walked into that room his mouth was shut and his eyes were opened. The most verbose of all the disciples had nothing to say. Spiritual maturity is not measured by one's ability to answer every question. It is signaled by ones humility to know that God is the answer when one has no answer.

Peter had been silent one other time. After the death of Jesus on the cross, Jesus appeared to the fishers on the shore. Peter jumped off the boat. This he did because he thought he had no explanation for his actions. He later discovered that God needed no explanation. He just needed his love and that was all the explanation that he wanted. Jesus asked: "Peter do you love me?"

Peter had nothing to say to those who gathered around Dorcas. He knew the look in their eyes. They had no explanation and he knew where to go. Perhaps he too was struck by the mystery of it all. Peter bowed and prayed. No account of his prayer is penned in scripture but every pastor, Christian, person of any faith, agnostic, atheist know what his prayer was: If there is a God; do you love us?

Before the funeral started, the most unlikely of people sat with one another. As the funeral progressed, the most amazing of colleague's friends and foes connected with one another and you could almost see the eyes of prejudice, ignorance and the ill-informed open. The vision of God expanded. The death of the extraordinary can change the life of the ordinary. Many people had attended a funeral or memorial service as a selfish person and have emerged as a crusader for the cause of Cancer, AIDS, Leukemia, Children's Charities, etc.. Their eyes were opened by the closing of the eyes of their friends who saw in us more than we saw in ourselves.

Though Dr. James Patterson's eyes were shut, he wasn't sleep. One could almost feel his presence in the church introducing and cajoling and persuading people to take a chance with one another. His eyes were shut but his presence was still alive. Death can take a body in a cruel and vicious manner but it cannot take a soul, erase a memory in others or stop the witness of a great man or woman.

Indeed the scriptures are a testament to this reality. Some people are weavers. Dorcas was a weaver. When Peter arrived at the house the people had gathered their various and sundry clothes and stood around the body. The clothes all had the burden of fitting the individual taste of the wearer and yet inevitably reflecting the voice of the weaver. This is why people such as Dr. James Patterson are so unforgettable. Some people can speak to your needs and yet, because they touched your life, influence the very ways in which you present yourself to the world. This is the legacy that special people leave us. It is also the reason for the special pain that their death cause us. It is the pathos behind the question of God's love and the silent vigil of the friends of Dorcas.

This vigil is what happens in memorial services and funerals. The questions, pain, anger and celebration fill the air. So, my mentor and friend did as Peter did. He did not preach but he prayed. If you are real: Do you love us?

Peter called the name – Dorcas! She rose. She was not gone! At the sound of her name from the lips of a disciple she rose. God was present and God loved them. God heard their cry and God cared about their pain. God would not let death be victorious. But, what about Dr. Patterson and all the other great men and women who were weavers? They were not healed and they died.

God answered both prayers. God loved them and loves us. Every eye that's shut ain't sleep and every good-bye ain't gone. When our bodies' fall exhausted in time we are not done. The scripture explains it this way:

> *Listen, I tell you a mystery: We will not all sleep,*
> *but we will all be changed in a flash, in the*
> *twinkling of an eye, at the last trumpet. For the*
> *trumpet will sound, the dead will be raised*
> *imperishable, and we will be changed. For the*
> *perishable must clothe itself with the imperishable*
> *and the mortal with immortality. When the*
> *perishable has been clothed with the imperishable,*

*and the mortal with immortality, then the saying
that is written will come true: "Death has been
swallowed up in victory.
"Where, O death is your victory?
Where, O death is your sting?"
The sting of death is sin, and the power of sin is
the law. But thanks be to God! He gives us the
victory through our Lord Jesus Christ. 1
Corinthians 15:57 (NIV)*

Our friends, family members and loved one are yet listening for a sound that will arouse them to reconnect us in a new dimension. Until then they are not simply sleep. Their voice, their relevance, their ministry continues for everyone who can open their hearts to the sound of their continued witness.

Death only wins when the pain of their loss causes us to become deaf to the things which made them passionate in their life. The memory and experience of them have left us a wardrobe tailored to the battles and celebrations of a future that you and I can live. If we become stuck at the point of their loss it is because we have become deaf to their life.

It is the memory of those who lived through the meanness and cruelty of a country scarred by A.I.D.S. that provided the vision and passion for those who established non-profits to provide care for people who are positive and living with HIV. The experience of lovers, husbands, wives, children, brothers and sister's who died without anyone to attend them, while people who should have loved them were rejecting them provide the pathos and passion of the Hospice movement. No, the vision of the extraordinary is not shut behind the eyelids of death. They are yet living in the hearts and minds of those who can faithfully hear the clarion call of their lives and give voice to the stories of lives well lived!

Note that Peter called everyone back into the room but that he especially wanted the widows to see the miracle. Dorcas was not a man and she had no "widow". But just because someone is not married; it doesn't mean that he or she does not have a widow or widower. This attentiveness to the widows was not about Dorcas but a message to all who felt that death had robbed them of power, position, and economic wealth. This is primarily what widowhood was about in the Bible. They were a protected category. Widows are the most impacted by death. They are the closest ones to the decease. They have the greatest struggle and the most to believe and to continue on.

When Peter called the people back in he wanted them to draw near and see what the Lord had done. Peter wanted them to know that God still loved them.

This is why the hope and assurance of the resurrection is so important. It is more than to empower us about-facing death. It is about empowering us to face life after someone has died. Jesus' disciples faced the same dilemma when he died. So then Jesus came to them and showed them that he yet lived. He empowered them to live in the vision and experience of his friendship with them. To the very disciple that stood over Dorcas Jesus said:

> *The third time he said to him, "Simon*
> *son of John, do you love me?" Peter was*
> *hurt because Jesus asked him the third*
> *time, "Do you love me?" He said, "Lord,*
> *you know all things; you know that I love*
> *you." Jesus said, "Feed my sheep."*
> *John 2:17 (NIV)*

The struggle of the hurt after the painful death of a friend is not easy. But it is worth the victory. Believing in the Love of God resurrects the gift of the life and presence of the one who has gone. Because of the resurrection: Every Eye that is shut ain't sleep. Every good-bye ain't gone.

Floyd Thompkins, Jr.

Questions and Exercises for Discussion

1. Either actively remember or tell the story of a Dorcas who died. Why was he or she so special?

2. What are some of the ways, ceremonies or rituals that you personally have to remember those who have died?

3. If you have had someone who has died of a long-term illness, what did that journey with them teach you about life and love? How did that journey with them change you and your faith? How do you teach those lessons to others?

4. How does sickness or disease breakdown the walls between people?

The Word of Their Testimony!

*Much people of the Jews therefore knew that he
was there: and they came not for Jesus' sake only,
but that they might see Lazarus also, whom he had
raised from the dead. But the chief priests consulted
that they might put Lazarus also to death; because
that by reason of him many of the Jews went away,
and believed on Jesus.*

` John 12:9-11(KJV)`

The residue of a miracle is a survivor. Survivors are the walking
embodiment of hope. Their testimonies supply the vocabulary of a
praise report. By simply relaying their experiences of the miraculous
they challenge the faithless. The terror that attend cancer and A.I.D.S,
just to name two diagnoses, topple at the sight of their chronic or
recovered condition. Survivors are powerful people

Lazarus was introduced to us as the head of the household of faith. He
was a favorite of Jesus. He and his house were especially comfortable
to Jesus. His house was especially well known to the people of his
town. Scripture records that Jesus and his disciples often stayed at his
house when they journeyed through town.

Yet, despite this appearance of favor, Lazarus became sick. His
relationship with Jesus neither protected him from this sickness nor did
it even give him a warning that it was on its way. Out of all his loyalty to
God, Lazarus was nevertheless singled out and successfully attacked.
It is clear that Lazarus' sisters were more than disturbed and then
angry with God.

But, while Mary and Martha's drama of anger and acceptance is well
chronicled, Lazarus is left silent. He simply is said to have died. His
identity within the scripture was simply this – someone who suffered
and died from a deadly disease. But, suddenly, because of a miracle
that no one saw coming he survived. But, what survived? Who was he
now? What had he become?

When Lazarus came forth out of his grave, the world had not changed.
But those at the graveside's understanding of the mysteries of life had

changed. Faith was different, Jesus was different and their relationship with God had all been changed. They were inspired and relived. But, Lazarus in his very continued existence became the touchstone of a great revelation of God.

When one survives a life threatening disease or sickness there is a strange shift in the atmosphere of the family. It seems as if these attacks, which threaten to obliterate the faith of the faithful, somehow have made their faith stronger. Suddenly, the questions and inquires of explanations, which were angrily shouted to God, are replaced with praise for God's healing power. Greater arrogance returns for the faithful. People of faith proclaim that they may not know why people get sick, but we certainly know who heals them. We know that the sick can be healed. It is stunning how quickly the angst of the faithful turns again into complacent confidence. Mary and Martha are not heard from again. Apparently, all was forgiven.

This is not the experience of the miracle survivor. The questions of why and the struggle to make sense of the experience and live in a new body persist. Often, this is so without mentors. The survivors have seen the good and bad in people who revealed themselves because they thought that they weren't going to be around. When people think they are speaking with a man or woman who is about to die they often take emotional risks to tell that person things which they would have never revealed otherwise. Some people show maudlin mercy, some demonstrate a gallows humor and others avoid the "dying" because of their own fear of their mortality.

As a survivor, one has seen people rally whom you thought would leave. Conversely, some people left who said they were going to be there to the bitter end. This is not some huge existential battle concerning the nature humanity. This is the battle to continue to forgive the people who left, accept the people who stayed and live with the knowledge that no one is predictable as one previously thought. This insight concerning this revelation of our human inconsistencies of friendship and fellowship can be disconcerting. One can be tempted to be cynical and depressed. Except, that the shear appreciation for one's continued existence overwhelms any tendency to be judgmental or resentful. Individual anger at one person is possible but, for the survivor, anger and resentment would be the epitome of ungratefulness.

In the midst of these monumental battles concerning life, faith and deep mysteries is the struggle to enter back into the ordinary of life. How does Lazarus, become ordinary again? How does he become Mary and Martha's elder brother? In fact, he will never be normal again. Having been defined previously as a man who was sick and then a dying man now, he would for the remainder of his life, be known as the man who died and yet lives – the survivor.

This distinction would become, in an odd sense, more isolating than any of his other previous experiences. In his community, while not everyone had been sick, only Lazarus had been resurrected. Others had been sicker than he. Others had been as close to Jesus as he. But, he alone was resurrected. What was so special about him? What had he done that others could emulate? The scriptures are silent as to whether Lazarus posed such questions. However, these are the questions that drove multitudes of people to travel to query him about his experience.

Indeed, there is a whole survivors' industry, which has sprung up around every disease. Survivors are asked to tell their stories to the delight and inspiration of the rest of us who are uncertain as to when and where we might face our own battles with mortality. For sure, we are genuinely happy for those who survive, but we also query them as to what they did. These questions are not only physical but also spiritual. We want to know what traditional or alternative medical regime, spiritual practice or religious practice did they engage.

So, too, with the people who came to visit Lazarus. Even the non-religious was curious. In fact, the scriptures comments that people came "not for Jesus sake only". While God might be unapproachable or inconceivable, a human being that is alive but should be dead is undeniable. Survivors, unlike faith are factual – this is the paradox.

The notion that the non-provable has evidence is disquieting to those who are not religious or faithful. So some come to see and hear the survivor out of curiosity. Some come out of disbelief and others out of a need for the affirmation of faith. This too, is the context of those who came to see Lazarus. The curious, the conceited, the critic and the septic were as interested in Lazarus as they were Jesus. All of these pilgrims encounter the same thing–a witness.

Survivors are not interested in convincing anyone of anything. They don't have an agenda of any kind. Survivors only tell the story of how they made it over. They are not argumentative or instructive. They tell their story with gratitude and total disregard to people's reaction. The survivors' power is that they tell the truth regardless of what you might think the facts are, or should be. In fact, if anything, their ability to rise above the facts of a situation and the stated odds of what should have happened is what makes them so fascinating. Perhaps this is why Lazarus words were not recorded. If you knew about the miracle – then you knew what the story was.

The witness of the story is universally accepted. But, the testimony of the witness is what causes issues and criticism. The "what happened" is seen as indisputable and unassailable. But, "the why" of the miracle is what is most controversial. The survivors' insistence on telling the audience that they had no control over the outcome of their miracle can draw downright anger from a crowd who has come to them seeking explanation. When the only explanation is the inexplicable it is more than heart breaking. It is challenging to the allusion of control. When the only explanation is the power and/or will of God, the religious and non-religious alike are challenged.

For the non-religious this explanation seems too simplistic and unresolved. They posit that, just as eyewitnesses are notoriously unreliable in the courtroom, so too are the witnesses to a miracle who are survivors. Of course, there is only one thing more unreliable in a courtroom than an eyewitness that is a jury member whose pre conceived notions might blind them to the truth that is presented to them. For the believer the explanation seems to lack denominational specificity and standards. The religious posit that witnesses who are survivors do not necessarily know enough theology to explain what has happened to them. Of course, the most ignorant people are those whose arrogant presumption of the importance about what they know keeps them from receiving a revelation because it doesn't fit in to their ideal of the way things must be.

Therefore, the testimony of the survivors can and does upset the systemic thinking of religious. These people have God confined in the web of his or her religious dogma. God operates within the prejudices, possibilities and positions of their religious universe alone. It is also upsetting to the non-religious whose worldview depends upon knowable and discoverable principles that can be controlled by human ingenuity. The testimony of the miraculous are not always accepted. In fact, like the reaction of the Pharisees in the scripture to Lazarus' testimony, it can be greeted with a desire to silence it.

The testimony of Lazarus represented the shift from the religious and cultural thoughts of the day. It didn't happen in Jerusalem. Lazarus' resurrection did not happen in the way expected by either the

Pharisees or the Sadducees. The miracle put Jesus at the center of the religious experience and not the Synagogue. It just wasn't kosher.

But, the thing about the witness and the testimony of the survivor is that people keep coming to hear and keep listening to the story. People want more than God to explain God's self to us.

No one believes what is said about God until someone can express what he or she has come to personally know about God. God doesn't need a witness but human beings do. After every resurrection Jesus asks a question to all who have experienced or witness the miraculous – will you be a witness? (Matthew 28:20) Let the Redeemed of the Lord say so! (Psalm 102:7)

But every survivor has questions that cause him or her to pause at this invitation. Every survivor struggles with the questions of why me? Only a truly arrogant person believes that he or she is more deserving of a miracle than all who have died before or since them. The weight of this can so pre-occupy some that it can become a burden of depression and threaten to destroy their legitimate joy. This is especially true if one has a chronic illness that threatens to yet destroy one's life. The routine of drugs, therapy and continued visits to the doctor can cause one to wonder as to what the purpose of continued existence in the face of having a healed body that nonetheless requires constant monitoring and care.

The experiences of one's life and the continued experience of one's will life change one's perspective of one's purpose. But it is only the perspective that has changed – not the purpose itself. Lazarus had a life before his sickness, disease and survival. We know that he was a leader of a family. His sisters loved him. He was a man of significant faith, as witness by his friendship with Jesus. Despite all of this what we remember him for and therefore his greatest contribution is as a survivor. In retrospect all of his previous existence was the building of a platform for his subsequent witness. He was always destined to be a witness.

It is not that Lazarus life before his experience was insignificant. In fact, it was a part of the miracle. But, the experience of the miraculous gave him the ability to expand his life far beyond the confines of his family, friends and circle of influence. The miracle of his survival elected him to become one of those human beings whose life was unforgettable and whose testimony is undeniable.

Lazarus no longer had the luxury of obscurity. Previously Lazarus was content to be a supporting actor in the faith of others. Before the miracle of his resurrection people came to his house to see Jesus. After the miracle, Lazarus had to adjust to becoming a main player. After his experience with a miracle, people journeyed to his house to see him. When Jesus resurrected Lazarus his life he became a religious celebrity. People wanted to see him and be in his presence hoping to become just like him- a miracle survivor.

One mention of the anniversary of a cancer-free diagnosis on Face book will bring the world to one's Face book wall. One description of oneself as living positive will bring the world to your doorstep. One mention of a congratulatory note in a friend's family newsletter will bring a note from a person that previously was unknown to a survivor. Whether one sees oneself as shy or unassuming the world cannot help itself. You are significant to others in an undeniable way. Without your permission and through no actions of your own, you have become a spokesperson concerning the mysteries of the universe.

The majority of people do not question your qualifications or your worthiness. You need not do so. Your story and your presence will change lives. You are relevant. This may or may not have been so jarring to Lazarus. But, to some it surely is. This is especially the case when you have survived or are surviving the odds of death from a disease or sickness with a stigma attached to it. It feels as though surviving is an outing. One's "status" colors everyone's perspective; causing doors to both open and close on both opportunities and relationships. For such people the "priest's" reaction–"let's seek to kill him"-is the overwhelming response.

But the reason for the priest reaction is the power of the witness to change their lives and minimize their power. More than anyone, the survivors of what was supposed to be a terminal illness from a disease or sickness that was supposed to be a part of God's punishment, challenges and debunks the religiously simple-minded who presume that God is as limited as their own conception of the universe. In the entire witness of the scriptures God healed no one from a plague that God supposedly set upon the people. By your very existence and your powerful testimony, you redeem God from the curse of the religious and the flawed logic or the fanatic.

Three years of miracles and what must have been dozens of sermons, were not enough to make some believe in Jesus. But the scripture says, because some saw and heard Lazarus, they believed. Marches, political movements, church services and theological/biblical treatise about religious prejudice are powerful but one meeting with a survivor and hearing their testimony can change a life and open up a minds, which after all the other efforts, had been left closed.

To the Christian, your miracle and survival are a part of the purpose of your life. It is also for the strengthening, correcting and enriching the faith of the faithful. Your weakness has made all of us stronger because through your experience we have expanded our sense of God's power and God's will to do the impossible. We come to know that at the extreme edges of our beliefs lies the opportunity of new revelations of God's power.

Lazarus just was when he wasn't suppose to be. Lazarus just answered the call and became a witness. Yes, it can be seen as forced courage or could be viewed as a forced privilege. To tell the story and let the world know of your experience does not lift you up. It lifts God above the traditional, mundane and predictable. And, if God were lifted up by a witness-God will draw all humanity unto God!

Questions and Exercises for Discussion

1. Are you or do you know a survivor? Find that person or those people and find out their story. If you are doing this exercise in a group setting ask survivors to tell their stories.

2. Does your church or community have a way to celebrate survival and healing? If not then think of a way to do so and help your church or community to celebrate their healing and their perseverance.

3. What are some other ways of celebrating healing and survivors?

We Shall Dance Again
An Ode to Eric

So Jeshua, his sons and his brothers, with Kadmiel, Binnui and Hodaviah, agreed to superintend the work of the temple of God. When the builders had laid the foundation of the sanctuary of God, the priest in fine linen came with trumpets, and the Levites the sons of Asaph, with cymbals, to praise God according to the ordinances of David, king of Israel: they chanted praise and thanksgiving to God, "For God is good, for God's love for Israel is everlasting."

And all the people shouted aloud the praises of God, since the foundations of the Temple of God had now been laid. True, many priests and Levites, many heads of families, who were then old and had seen with their own eyes the earlier Temple on its foundations, wept aloud, but many others raised their shouts of joy. And nobody could distinguish the shouts of joy from the sound of the people's weeping; for the people shouted so loudly that noise could be heard far away.
Ezra 3:9-13

The tears will not cease. The crying may stop, but the weeping will never be over. The loss is too great to recede with the onslaught of death, healing or a cure. Too many did not live to see this day. Sickness and disease have done their job too well for people to simply rise and resume life. The fragility of life, the brutality of death and the sovereignty of God have unleashed their awesome power too brilliantly upon the earth to simply let the disease, suffering, struggles and noble witnesses slip away into the nether worlds of our memories. Such carnage that the disease has already caused and promises to create is unrelentingly with us. The shy of the world of the future is grey with grief. The earth of the present is wet beneath our feet with the tears of sorrow. All things previously solid in our lives have become softer and more fertile for change and growth.

No corner of the world has been spared and none will escape this pain. The world will never be the same. The disease and sickness have attempted to steal our most precious gift we have–joy. Death is not the issue; we have all seen singular death, but this terror has brought

77

death and vulnerability such as we seldom has seen. It also has brought plagues–paranoia, fear, poverty, abandonment and meanness have spread around the world. Nations would not let the sick enter their borders. The police put gloves on their hands and cover their mouths with mask before they would protect or arrest the suffering. The churches avoided their responsibility for compassion by blaming the dying and excruciating suffering on God's wrath without God's permission. Sex became a dangerous and dirty act of horror. Children were born with death in their bodies. Schools let ignorance go one the rampage too long before they educated the young to be compassionate and understanding.

What is most unforgiveable of all is that my people, of a dark hue and complexion, may suffer the worst before it is over. Those in the mother country and their strange cousins here in the "land of the free and the home of the brave" have been, and are becoming, its worst victims. True, we are no less or no more deserving of this plague than anyone else, but we've been so acquainted with grief and so locked in the mortal embrace with poverty so many times in our history, that I'd hoped that this horror would not find us an alluring enough target to infect. Instead, America, when we were already fending off the self-inflicted genocidal attacks of murder, drugs, and the legal homicide of the death penalty, this killer came along and joined the feeding frenzy. It is just another reason for African American women, men and children to die needlessly and unexplainably.

I cannot write its name because I cannot give it the honor of its infamy. Its name alone embarrasses those of us in the African American Church tradition. As our preachers slowly died and our sons and daughters sadly slipped away from us, I and my colleagues in the ministry only prayed and judged. It took too long for us to come down off our pulpits to weep with those who wept, and teach the tools of survival to those who could be saved. Because we could not say the word condom or speak of sex or crusade against dirty needles, many died. If we are going to extol the great power of the Black Church's pulpit, we also must accept its responsibility. We must hear the sobs of mothers whose sons were not perfect and whose troubles began long before the disease, and consider whether we did all that we could to save them. Yes, ultimately God will have to shoulder the grief, anger and accusations for this horror, but we too will have to account for our actions.

AIDS-yes, we must call its name, although we must be on guard, lest this label replace the names of our friends and loved ones who died of this deadly disease. Neither can we forget the mothers and fathers, sisters and brothers, who grieved and struggled to regain a lost sense of themselves. Finally, we cannot forget those who are living with the HIV virus. For the sake of all of these whom AIDS has attacked, we cannot allow the disease its greatest victory, which is to stop the dance of joy and love which is the very privilege of human existence.

Such was the issue in the case of the Jewish people's captivity. Jeremiah wrote of this time period as one in which "the old ones became weary and the young ones utterly lost hope." When Nebuchadnezzar took the nation Israel into captivity, he followed a policy of taking away the best and the brightest young people of Israel. The people who remained had no hope in their future.

Unlike the past, which is nothing more than the shadows of lives refracted through the prisms of our collective memories, the future is but a dark fertile unknown. If has no shape or definition. Consequently, the future is both ominous and exciting. It is only when one peers into the faces of the young that the future takes on any definition at all. The future, therefore, resides in the present, through the twinkle in the eyes of the young. When these eyes are prematurely closed by death, as with disease, or they simply vanish, as with the offspring of the children of Israel, one is left to face the void of the future with only the counsel of the fear and pessimism of a childless present.

Left in Judah, the people of Israel were without the resources to conjure up a notion of a future, which was better than their present. Cruelly, their one consistent source of hope, their temple, was also destroyed. Of course, temples of faith are seldom left standing when the future has been destroyed.

God can be worshipped without a temple. Prayer can be offered to God in something other than a temple. However, a temple is not primarily about worship or praise; it is about witness and testimony. A temple is a storehouse of the present for the future. Because the future is so inaccessible for the present, it is not clear whether the current human achievements will be of any value to the future. What is so critical today may be obsolete by tomorrow. However, because the future resides in the children of the present, the only thing that is for sure is the people who inherit the future will be like us.

What is known is that the lessons of perseverance, the testimonies of the miraculous, the witnesses as to the trustworthiness of God, and the stories as to the power of love will always be in vogue. No matter what the future holds this legacy will never be passé. The stories of "how we got over" will endure for an eternity. Tragedy and triumphs will always characterize the human experience.

The people of Israel had prepared a special place for the most precious supplies in the storehouse of faith. In the Holy of Holies, at the center of the temple, the Ark of the Covenant resided. There the books of Mosses lay, in which the story of their liberation from the hands of Pharaoh was told. There also lay the symbols of triumph: Aaron's budding rod, a shofar, and the Torah. Besides these symbols, the Ark also held the testimonies of the great battles of Israel. Before these treasures, in great appreciation of the legacy of faith to be left to the future, the people of Israel danced. By its very existence, the temple signaled God's care for a people. It allowed the old ones to "die easy" because their legacy was enshrined in the testimonies of the temple. The temple allowed the young ones to dance joyously, because they were not alone. The prophets, priest, widows and orphans were always with them as long as they had a temple. This is what a temple is for—a storehouse of faith waiting for the children of the future.

However, when the children were gone and their testimony of God's faithfulness seemed in doubt, the children of Israel had no need for a temple. Their world had been laid waste. They were filled with anger, mixed with grief. They could no longer dance and worship. They could no longer believe that God was either fair or just. Only mourning and moaning were left. Jeremiah wrote:

My grief is beyond healing; my heart is sick within me, Hark the cry of the daughter of my people from the length and breadth of the land: "Is the Lord not in Zion? Is her King not in her?"...

"The harvest is past, the summer is ended, and we are not saved!" For the wound of the daughter of my people is in my heart wounded, I mourn, and dismay had taken hold of me. Is there no balm in Gilead? Is there no physician there? Why then has the health of the daughter of my people not been restored? O that my head were waters, mine eyes a fountain of tears. Then I might weep day and night for the slain daughter of my people! Jeremiah 8: 18 – 9:1

Stunned and shocked, they were wounded in a place so deep that words have never visited it. Their hurt defied description. Questions with no answers were left to them for almost a whole generation. The world made no sense to them. In a very real sense the veil of tears, which covers one's eyes when children and the young die or disappear, obscures God also. This is especially true when a generation is lost.

AIDS and the captivity of Judah were both phenomenon which obscure God. How can the temple stand in the wake of such awful loss? In fact, whenever one loses a loved one by a slow lingering disease, the temple of faith threatens to crumble because its testimonies are all called into question. Therefore, the attacks of doubt, cynicism, righteous indignation and sneering ridicule crumble the once great walls of the temple. The enemy last attack is complete. Why participate in the congregation of the temple, praises the Lord, or even believe in a place, a vision and a God that have failed.

Astonishingly, the scriptures seem to suggest that God concurs with the temple's destruction. The prophetic literature of this time period is filled with references to Judah's failures of compassion and grace. The prophets even pleaded with the nation to change before the impending doom came upon them:

Hear the Word of the Lord, all you people of Judah who come through these gates worship the Lord. This is what the Lord Almighty, the God of Israel, says: "Reform your ways and your actions, and I will let you live in this place.

"Do not trust in the deceptive words and say the temple of the Lord, the temple of the Lord! If you really change your ways and your actions and deal with each other justly, if you do not oppress the alien, fatherless, or the widow and do not shed innocent blood in the place, and if you do not follow other gods to your own harm, then I will let you live in this place, in the land I gave your forefathers for ever and ever..."
(Jeremiah 7:2-7)

A nation that had known oppression and discovered its identity in the crucible of persecution had lost sight of whom and what they were. The temple had therefore lost its meaning long before its walls came tumbling down.

As to whether God brought the marauding enemy of destruction to Judah or "allowed it to happen" is a matter of interpretation and conjecture for the modern reader. But, what is clear from the biblical text is that the scribes, who wrote about these events from the other side of the catastrophe, discerned grace in their occurrence. They also ascribed to God responsibility for their defeat. They heard from the Lord a willingness to be blamed for the pain and suffering of the people. Whatever else the God of the temple was, this God was not a coward. As God would demand the praise for causing the victories, God also demanded the blame for causing the defeat.

It is left up to every believer to come to peace with the true God, the one who will not flee the whirlwind of our doubts or shrink away from the power of our disillusionment. God is only real if God is constantly with us, even when we do not believe, cannot understand and cannot testify. The biblical witness to the character of God never lets God's hands or heart be disengaged from ours. Death, destruction, AIDS, cancer, or natural disasters never happen apart from God. God may not always give us an explanation, but every believer has the right to ask questions. God is much more durable than the temple.

Just as God cannot escape the passion and power of doubt and anguish, neither can the temple community. Jeremiah, Ezekiel and other prophets were painfully clear that more than God held responsibility for the desolation of the temple and the destruction of their people. Those who were in the congregation of the temple warranted questioning. It was clear that their lack of moral vision and compassion and their participation in the forces of oppression were somewhat responsible for the desolation and destruction of their temple. It is not simply the outside forces or the future of their God, but their own failures. How long had the prophets cried to them to call for justice, uphold morality and show compassion? And they would not heed their call. So their sons and daughters, and loved ones suffered. They were guilty of a crime of faithfulness. Their grief was increased by their own prophets who would not let them escape from their faith. The weeping and wailing were for themselves as well as the dead and the loss of the temple.

The weeping and wailing was for those who have died from AIDS have not yet reached such splendid proportions. We are still seeking to blame the dead, indict God alone, or simply mourn the exodus of the young and vibrant from our churches. Still, we have not come to grips with the fact that we eroded our own testimonies of faith with our indifference, indecision and inability to be engaged in the struggle for justice. We have forgotten the plaintive prayer of the "Negro National Anthem":

Let our feet stray from the places of our God, where we met thee; lest our hearts drunk with the wine of the world we forget thee; Shadowed beneath thy hand may we forever stand, true to our God, true to our native land.

Intoxicated with the gains of a civil rights movement and enchanted by a rising sense of our own political importance, we forgot the meaning of a temple. We allowed the Eric's of an entire generation to slide perilously into the onslaught of our destructive indifference.

Eric was a child of the church. His mother is a pillar of the community. Her testimonies and financial resources helped lay the foundations of the temple. Nevertheless, she could not shield her child from the wandering pack of wolves that inhabit the streets. He was not terribly strong, but he was also not unusually weak. He was a young man who, more than most, could hear the harmonies and melodies of life, which surround us all. As assuredly as his melodious voice could fill up a church, his ever-so-vibrant spirit could literally overwhelm a room. He needed the temple because he was ultimately attacked by heroine, crack and, finally, AIDS.

When he needed the temple to have an anti-drug ministry-there was none. When he needed the temple ministry to talk to him in adolescence about sex–there was none. When he needed to know that his mother was being cared for while he lay dying in the hospital – try as she might, his mother could not conceal the fact that those in the temple had abandoned both him and her. No, the temple was not responsible for the virus, which infected Eric, but it was nevertheless implicated in his death.

So at his funeral, the temple folk showed up en mass to mourn and cry. By now their weeping was for their own sons and daughters. They wept in white. They wept because Eric was not the only black man and woman who died. It is now evident that drugs, AIDS, murder, racist attacks, and an unjust criminal justice system have brought to the African American community genocide. The African American men and women who have escaped the slaughter have been deported to college, and then stay in a far off land, never to return again. Yes, they wept loudly, and we weep loudly and mourn.

As with the old ones who wept in the temple ceremony, the weeping was not all about what God had done. We wept because of what we had done. So, the exhaustion of grieving leaves us to ask the question: Will the young who are still alive and the old who have disappointed ever feel like dancing the dance of joy again? Is the temple doomed, like so many other American institutions of our times, to lie in waste? Factories have closed; the railroad has given way to the airplane. What will the Black Church give way to? Will the seduction of the electronic church or the growing movement of a spiritual existence without Jesus, God or a community of believers rises to take the place of the Black Church?

Similar questions hung in the hearts of Judah as they grieved their lost and lived in the captivity of Babylon. But the answer was not in Babylon, it was where it had always been–in the Testimonies of the temple. Ezra had hidden away the Books of Mosses until the temple would be rebuilt. As a priest, the believed that a temple, a house of worship, and a God to believe in were essentials for a human life. Ezra also believed that the temple was established by divine edict. It had to be rebuilt, not so much by human design but by God's will.

The explanation for God's forthright involvement in humanity is that God has an unassailable desire that humanity be saved from itself and from the things that seek to destroy us. From the creation, out of love, to the redemption of the law and grace, God has declared a will for salvation. The whirlwind of praise in song and dance in the temple is not just a celebration of God, but also an expression of the joy of life. If human beings can dance, sing and shout after a tragedy then, perhaps, we will have learned something from it. The tears of the past will provide the nourishment for our future.

Eric's death and the death of all sons and daughters and loved one is only understandable if there is a new temple that emerge : one built upon a new foundation of compassion, openness and resolve. Both in the book of Ezra and Nehemiah there is an emergence of a new nation built upon the old testimonies of grace and compassion. In neither book does the weeping stop, but it is joined by a great shout of joy. In the new births and the rise of another generation of young people, the future and the present meet. The Eric's are gone but the new children have arrived. So the weeping over the past becomes a part of the shouting of the present. Would that we never forget the suffering, and that we never completely overcome our participation in the carnage. Rather, as James Weldon Johnson wrote, let us:

Sing a song full of the faith that the dark past has taught us; sing a song full of the hope that the present has brought us; facing the rising sun of our new day begun, let us march on till victory is won.

Thank you for taking the time to read this book. I invite you to share your feeling and feedback about this book by going to the website wwwbythepoolofbethesda.com and join the blog discussion, leave your experience in reading the book or purchase another book as a gift for a friend. You can also email me directly at floyd@bythepoolofbethesda.com

Join me in creating a place to spiritually support the healing process. Thanks again for your time and contribution, both in reading and sharing your thoughts and experiences through the blogs.

God bless you and keep you,

Rev. Floyd Thompkins, Jr.

www.ingramcontent.com/pod-product-compliance
Lightning Source LLC
Chambersburg PA
CBHW062023040426
42447CB00010B/2113